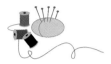

Embellishments for Adventurous Sewing

Creative Publishing
international

Copyright © 2013 Creative Publishing international, Inc.

First published in the United States of America by Creative Publishing international, Inc., a member of Quayside Publishing Group
400 First Avenue North
Suite 300
Minneapolis, MN 55401
1-800-328-3895
www.creativepub.com

ISBN: 978-1-58923-731-5

10 9 8 7 6 5 4 3 2 1

Library of Congress Cataloging-in-Publication Data Available

Copy Editor: Peggy Wright

Proofreader: Karen Ruth

Book Design: Diana Boger

Cover Design: Creatvie Publishing international

Page Layout: Leslie Haimes

Illustrations: Diana Boger

Photographs: Nancy S. J. Langdon and Kevin May

Printed in China

Embellishments for Adventurous Sewing

Master Appliqué, Decorative Stitching,

and Machine Embroidery through

Easy Step-by-step Instruction and Fun projects

Carol Zentgraf

Creative Publishing
international

Contents

Introduction.................................. 6

Getting Started

Supplies 10

Decorative Stitching

Techniques 20

Decorative Stitching Projects:
- Tablet Cover 34
- Globe Trotting Tote 38
- Monogrammed Table Topper............. 40

Appliqué

Techniques 46
Raw-edge Appliqué 48
Dimensional Appliqué............................ 49
Reverse Appliqué 50

Appliqué Projects:
- Appliquéd Chair Cushion 54
- Raw-edge-appliqué Pillow 60
- Dimensional-appliqués Throw 64

Trim Time

Techniques..................................... 72

Trim Time Projects:
- Embellished Jacket 86
- Embellished Motifs Pillow 88
- Pillow with Trim Design.................... 90

Fabric Manipulation

Techniques...................................... 94

Projects:
- Trapunto Floor Pillow 110
- Yo-yo Door Hanger 114
- Textured-blocks Wall Hanging........... 116

Artistic Elements

Techniques..................................... 126

Projects with Artistic Elements:
- Bleach-motifs Floor Pillow 134
- Nature's Harmony Wall Canvas 138
- Painted, Etched, and Dyed Scarf 140

Credits and Sources..................... 142
About the Author 143
Index 144

Introduction

I have always loved creating art! As a child, I always had a pencil and sketchbook in hand or used a paintbrush to embellish any surface I was allowed to paint. Now my art medium of choice is fabric. I love to sew, and fabric is the perfect surface for a wide variety of embellishments. Why simply make a pillow with a pretty print fabric when you can do so much more? You can embellish the fabric's design with stitching, beads, or buttons or create a trapunto effect. And that's just the beginning. You can personalize your décor or spice up your wardrobe in SO many ways with creative embellishments.

Through the pages of this book, you'll discover how to incorporate the built-in decorative stitches on your machine and digitized embroidery designs into your projects and add details with bobbin work, heirloom stitches, and free-motion stitching. We'll explore different types of appliqué, from those made traditionally with satin-stitched edges to fun dimensional appliqués made with dyed and boiled wool felt or appliqués made from a photo using printable, water-soluble stabilizer. Or use trims; the possibilities are almost endless. Have fun creating edge or surface embellishments with fabric tubes and water-soluble stabilizer, enhance the fabric's motifs or create your own designs with couched cording, or give definition to edges and seams with piping or cording. Add flat or dimensional designs to garments and accessories using ribbon, fringe, and decorative trims. Go

wild and accent a neckline or the fabric's design with buttons or beads, or use grommets, eyelets, or zippers in decorative and unconventional ways. Or you can use fabric manipulation—one of my favorite techniques. With it, you can make fabulous fabric even better by changing or enhancing its texture. Use trapunto to showcase motifs or add surface interest with gathers, pleats, tucks, or slits. Last but not least, I can't resist the lure of paints, dyes, and even bleach when it comes to embellishing fabric. Call upon your inner artist and be adventurous (and maybe a little messy) by adding color or taking it out or even by etching fibers to create a design. If paints and dyes don't appeal to you, you can wear your artist's cap and combine fabrics, photo transfers, trims, and more to make a fabric collage.

The techniques mentioned are just some of the ones featured in this book, and step photography and clear instructions accompany all of them. This book also includes 15 projects to get you started, and you'll be sure to think of many others during your adventurous sewing. Have fun and remember that best of all, embellishing is fun, and there really isn't a right or wrong way to add creative touches. While I may not still be that girl who sat cross-legged on the floor to paint, mixing colors on her knee, I still get the same thrill out of seeing a surface transformed by embellishment, and I think you will too!

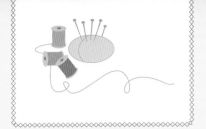

GETTING STARTED

If you are an adventurous sewer, chances are good that you
love fabrics and trims as well as all of the wonderful threads,
beads, buttons, and other artistic accents that await you!
Each piece of fabric offers so much potential for embellishment,
and you can try so many exciting techniques.

Supplies

FABRICS

Do you have a fabric stash? If you've been sewing for a while, you probably do—that beautiful silk fabric that caught your eye, an amazing hand-dyed or hand-woven fabric, wool with a luscious texture, or a cotton or decorator fabric with a fabulous print that was too good to pass up.

Or maybe you fell in love with the charm of some vintage fabrics or embroidered linens. Well, it's time to discover the creative potential of some of those fabrics when you embellish them, and you'll be surprised that even some of your shopping mistakes can take on a whole new look with the right embellishment technique. If you're a beginner and don't have a stash yet, don't worry; you will build one soon enough. The main thing to remember, whether you're pulling from your stash or ready to head out on a fabric shopping spree, is to use fabrics that are suitable for the embellishment technique you're planning. While a wide range of fabrics are suitable for many embellishment techniques, the following fabrics are leading players in this book:

Natural-fiber fabrics such as wool, cotton, linen, and silk are good choices for many embellishment techniques. Lighter weights of these fabrics are especially ideal for fabric-manipulation techniques like pleats, ruffles, ruching, or tucks where sharp creases or shape retention is important. Look for them in a wide variety of colors, prints, weights, and interesting textures.

Hand-woven and hand-dyed fabrics add interesting colors, designs, and textures to your projects. Look for them at quilt and fabric expos or from online sources.

Wool felt, real or faux suede, and other nonwoven fabrics will not ravel and don't require an edge finish. Use them for cut-out areas, appliqués, binding, borders, and dimensional embellishments. They are also ideal for cut strips, loops, and projects that showcase the seam allowances on the outside of the project.

Upcycled fabrics can be fun to use and eco-friendly at the same time. Consider felting wool sweaters or garments to create a dense fabric that won't ravel to make scarves or throws that you can embellish with appliqués or stitching. Or recycle cotton or silk garments by cutting them into pieces to use for crazy quilting or fabric collages.

Embroidered vintage linens pair beautifully with new fabrics and add a touch of hand embroidery to your designs.

Multi-Purpose Cloth is a canvas-like cloth that has substantial body and is available in white as well as 12 colors. It can be cut with regular scissors, sewn, punched, and folded and is easy to sew, paint, and embroider. You can use it as a foundation for fabric designs to create floor cloths, wall hangings, table runners, and many other projects.

THREADS, YARNS, AND TRIMS

This is where the fun begins, with an almost endless array of gorgeous threads, yarns, and trims that awaits your creative machine stitching. Use them for surface embellishments or edge finishes.

Decorative Threads

Available in a wide range of colors, thread types, and weights, decorative threads are beautiful for surface stitching, and you also can use some for construction. Consider the thread's attributes when making your selection. Thread labels give the type and weight; the higher the number, the finer the thread.

Cotton thread is available in a wide range of solid and blended colors, has a matte finish, and is usable for construction as well as for decorative stitching. Use 30-wt. cotton thread for general sewing and decorative stitching or heavier 12-wt. cotton thread for more coverage and bobbin work. Because cotton thread is spun, it's important to use good-quality, long-staple thread to prevent breakage and excess lint.

Rayon thread is also available in a wide range of beautiful colors and has a high luster. Look for it in 30-wt. or 40-wt. machine-embroidery threads and heavier decorative threads. It isn't as strong as cotton or polyester thread, making it ideal for decorative stitching or couching but not for construction.

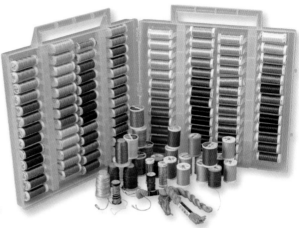

Polyester thread is strong and colorfast. You can use it for construction, embroidery, and decorative stitching. Use 40-wt. for embroidery or quilting and 60-wt. for bobbin thread, appliqué, or any technique where you want strong stitches that are barely visible.

Metallic thread can add glitz to your decorative stitching. It is available in weights ranging from fine to heavy and in a variety of metallic finishes. For best results, use a metallic needle and experiment with the metallic thread before stitching your project. You may need to lower the tension, reduce the speed, or use a vertical spool pin if breakage occurs.

Pearl cotton is a thick thread that's available in several weights and in an array of beautiful colors. It is too heavy to machine stitch with the needle but is perfect for bobbin work and couching.

Yarns and Other Trims

Add interest to surface embellishments or edges by incorporating yarn, cording, ribbon, and other trims.

When couched in place, yarn can add color, dimension, and interest to surface embellishments. Be sure the yarn you use is fine enough that the widest setting of your machine's zigzag stitch can cross over it or plan to hand-stitch it in place.

You can machine stitch ribbon and other flat trims to the fabric surface or insert it in seams. You can pleat or ruffle it for surface or edge finishes and also use it to create dimensional appliqués, loops, and straps.

As surface embellishment, you can couch or hand-stitch cording and other dimensional trims in place. You can cover cotton cording with fabric to make piping or tubes, and some dimensional trims have a lip that you can sew into a seam.

Buttons, grommets, and zippers have a practical side, but look beyond their intended uses and apply them to fabric surfaces as decorative embellishments.

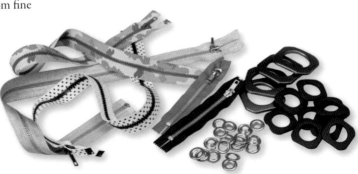

SEWING MACHINE NEEDLES

Selecting the right needle for the fabric, thread, and stitch type can prevent all kinds of frustrations—broken needles and thread, holes or snags in fabric, puckered seams, uneven stitches, and more.

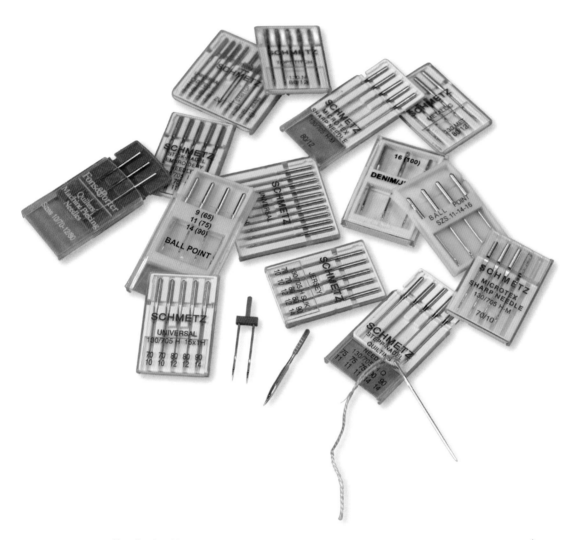

Needle size. Needle packaging usually lists the needle's size, giving two numbers that range from size 60/8–120/20, with the needle size increasing with the number. In general, use sizes 60/8–75/11 for lightweight fabrics, size 80/12 or 90/14 for medium-weight fabrics, size 100/16 for heavyweight fabrics, and sizes 110/18 and up for very heavy fabrics.

Needle types. Needles vary according to the shape of the point, the eye's shape, and the needle's thickness. Select the needle type that best suits the kind of fabric you will be sewing or the stitching technique you have in mind; then pick the needle size that is appropriate for the fabric's weight and type of thread.

General Purpose Needles

Needle Type	Sizes/Features	Use/Fabrics
Universal Point	60/8–120/19. The slightly rounded point is rounded enough for stitching knits yet pointed enough for stitching woven fabrics.	General stitching on woven and knit fabrics in wide range of weights.
Ball Point	70/10–100/16. The point is more rounded than the Universal point.	Needle slides between yarns of knits instead of piercing them, eliminating risk of snags or holes. Good for spandex and interlock knits that run easily. These needles are also good for creating even stitches on heavy knits.
Sharp/Microtex	60/8–90/14. Has a sharp point and narrow shaft.	Ideal for very straight stitching, topstitching, heirloom sewing, and pin tucks. Use on smooth, finely woven fabrics like microfibers, silk, chintz, and lightweight faux suede.

Specialty Needles

Needle Type	Sizes/Features	Use/Fabrics
Denim/Jeans	70/10–110/18. The stiff, thick, strong shank resists breaking and has a very sharp point.	Use for stitching multiple layers of fabric and tightly woven fabrics like denim, canvas, and cotton duck.
Hemstitch/Wing	100/16 and 120/19. The shaft features a wing on each side and produces a decorative hole.	Use for hemstitching, heirloom stitching, openwork, and other decorative stitches on tightly woven fabrics such as linen and batiste.
Leather	80/12–110/18. Has a wedge-shaped point.	Use to create strong seams on leather, suede, vinyl, and other nonwoven fabrics. Do not use on woven or knit fabrics.
Machine Embroidery	70/10–90/14. The large eye and special scarf protect the thread while stitching dense designs at high speed and prevent shredding and breaking.	Use for machine embroidering with rayon and specialty threads. Use on any fabric.
Metallic	80/12. The eye, which is larger than that of a machine- embroidery needle, enables stitching with heavier threads. The large groove and specially designed scarf protect delicate threads and prevent shredding during stitching.	Use with metallic thread on any fabric.
Quilting	75/11 and 90/14. Has a sharp, tapered point.	Use for stitching through multiple fabric layers and intersecting seams. Use for piecing quilts and quilting layers together.
Stretch	75/11 and 90/14. The deep scarf allows the bobbin hook to get closer to the needle's eye and prevents skipped stitches on fine, lightweight, knit fabrics.	Use for swimwear, fabrics containing spandex, synthetic suedes, silk jersey, and other elasticized lightweight knits.
Topstitch	80/12, 90/12, and 100/16. Has an extra-sharp point. The extra-large eye and large groove accommodate heavy topstitching thread or double strands of all-purpose thread.	Use for straight, accurate stitching with heavier threads on variety of fabrics.
Twin	1.6/70 and 4.0/100. Has two needle shafts on a crossbar that extends from a single shank, and the available needle types include universal point, denim, hemstitch/wing, machine embroidery, and metallic. Also is available with one hemstitch/wing needle paired with one universal needle.	Use for stitching two parallel rows at once for pin tucks, heirloom stitching, hems, and decorative stitches. Use on fabric appropriate to the needle's type. Select closely-spaced needles for lighter fabric weights and needles spaced farther apart for heavier fabrics.

SPECIALTY SEWING-MACHINE FEET

Think beyond basic sewing-machine feet and maximize your machine's potential when you use specialty feet. From applying cording to attaching a button, many specialty feet exist, each designed for a specific purpose. Although the names may vary according to the manufacturer, the following feet or similar ones are ideal for embellishment techniques.

1. ADJUSTABLE ZIPPER AND PIPING FOOT. This foot is narrow and adjustable from the throat plate. Use it when you to stitch closer to the zipper's teeth or the edge of piping or welting than is possible with a standard zipper foot.

2. BINDING FOOT. This foot features a funnel guide for bias tape that wraps around the fabric's edge. Feed bias tape through the guide to bind a fabric's edge easily.

3. BRAIDING FOOT. This foot has a flat opening in the front for inserting narrow flat trims. Use it with a zigzag stitch to couch on braids, ribbons, tapes, cords, and more for surface embellishments.

4. CLEAR FOOT. This foot allows you to clearly see marked stitching lines or seams. Use it for many techniques including appliqué, edge stitching, topstitching, and decorative stitching.

5. CORDING FOOT. Cording feet feature holes on the front of the foot designed for feeding fine cords or decorative threads. The number of holes can vary from one to seven, depending on the foot. Use it to couch one or multiple cords or decorative threads in place for surface designs or to embellish seams, edges, or other trims.

6. ECHO STITCHING FOOT. The design of this round clear foot aids in stitching evenly-spaced parallel rows. It has markings on the foot to guide you in maintaining an even distance from the previous row of stitching. Use it for free-motion echo stitching or echo stitching with feed dogs.

7. EDGE JOINING FOOT. This foot features a guide for the precise joining of two fabrics or a fabric and flat trim. Use it to attach lace or other edge trim to a fabric's edge, to piece hemmed or nonwoven edges, to produce edge stitching, or to create pin tucks.

8. EMBROIDERY FOOT. Designed for digitized machine embroidery, this foot features a large opening that allows the needle to move freely in any direction and enables easy viewing of the stitches. It rests lightly on the surface so the fabric moves easily beneath the needle.

9.

10.

11.

12.

13.

14.

15.

16.

17.

9. FRINGE FOOT. This foot features a raised area in the center of the foot that creates a loop. Use it with a wide zigzag stitch and leave thread looped or cut loops in the center to make fringe.

10. GATHERING FOOT. You can use this foot just for gathering fabric or for gathering fabric and attaching the gathered edge to a flat fabric. Use with lightweight to medium-weight fabrics.

11. NONSTICK FOOT. The bottom of this foot is coated with material that will not stick to fabrics such as leather, vinyl, plastic, and other fabrics that tend to stick to a metal foot.

12. PEARLS AND SEQUINS FOOT. This foot has a groove in the front that is wide enough for threaded beads, sequins, or rounded cords up to 4 mm. Feed the trim through the groove and couch it in place with a zigzag stitch and transparent thread. You also can use this foot to make or attach piping.

13. PINTUCK FOOT. This foot has multiple grooves in the front to produce perfect pin tucks or corded pin tucks. Use it on lightweight fabric with a twin needle and stitch slowly for best results.

14. RUFFLER FOOT. This foot features a blade with teeth that catches the fabric and moves it forward into evenly-spaced tucks or gathers, the spacing of which you can adjust. Use it to gather an edge or create ruffles.

15. ¼" (6 mm) PIECING FOOT. Designed for straight stitching only, this foot features a small opening for the needle and edges marked for precise ⅛" (3 mm) or ¼" (6 mm) seams. Use it for piecing, edge stitching, topstitching, or any stitching where precision is especially important.

16. OPEN TOE FOOT. This foot features a large opening on the front to give you wide visibility. Use it for free-motion stitching and quilting and other techniques where you need needle visibility.

17. WALKING FOOT. The feed dogs on this foot move at the same rate as the machine's lower feed dogs to feed the fabric evenly. Use it for fabrics that may otherwise shift such as velvet, vinyl, leather, and multiple quilting layers.

OTHER SUPPLIES AND NOTIONS

In addition to standard sewing supplies like your sewing machine, scissors, pins, rotary cutter, rulers, cutting mats, and pressing equipment, you may want to have other supplies on hand before you begin your embellishment projects. Some are necessary, and others, like handy portable cutting and sewing mats or tube turners, will just make your life easier.

Interfacings, Stabilizers, and Fusible Web

Interfacings and stabilizers are important components of many embellishment projects and are available in a variety of types.

Manufacturers have designed some stabilizers specifically to back fabric for machine embroidery and decorative stitches. These are usually available in rolls or sheets sized to fit machine-embroidery hoops, and your choices include iron-on, tear-away, cut-away, wash-away, heat-away, and permanent. Wash-away stabilizer is available in clear, plastic-like or fabric-like fabrications. You can use the clear type on top of a fabric with a nap to prevent the stitches from sinking into the nap, and this type is also perfect for sandwiching overlapping threads, yarns, ribbon, and fibers for stitching to create free-motion thread lace, scarves, and other surface or edge designs. Fabric-like wash-away stabilizer is ideal for cutwork and other applications.

Other interfacings and stabilizers are wider and available by the yard (meter) in fusible or nonfusible fabrications and for a wide range of purposes and fabric weights. They prevent the fabric from stretching or distorting during cutting and stitching or during the addition of heavier embellishments like buttons, beads, or trims. You also can use fusible stabilizers to position fabric pieces for collage or contemporary crazy quilting or use very heavyweight stabilizers to add structure or shape.

Fusible web is available in sheets, by the yard (meter), and as tape. The sheets and yardage feature a paper backing on both sides. They are ideal for transferring patterns to fabric for appliqués and for fusing the appliqués to the background fabric. Some fusible webs are double-stick, allowing you to reposition the fabric as desired before pressing. Fusible web tape features a paper backing on one side and is perfect for hemming edges, applying trims, and more. Fusible web is permanent after pressing, and you can stitch through it.

Temporary Spray Adhesive

Sometimes it's easier to spray the back of the pieces of fabric with adhesive than it is to pin them in place, and this spray (not pictured) allows you to reposition them as needed.

Fabric Tube Turners

These tools definitely fall into the "making your life easier" category. Use the guide to stitch precisely sized bias tubes from 3/16"–1⅛" (0.5–2.9 cm)-wide; then easily turn them right side out using the metal cylinders and wires. You also can use the tools to fill fabric tubes with cording for surface designs or to make piping.

Cotton Cording

Available in several widths, cording is also referred to as piping or filler cord. You can cover it with fabric to make decorative cording, piping or welting. One of my favorite products for finishing an edge with cording is fusible cording with a lip, available in a smaller size for piping or a larger size for welting.

Basting Tape

Self-adhesive, double-sided basting tape (not pictured) features paper backing on one side. It is the best choice for securing layers of fabrics like faux suede, faux leather, and other fabrics where pin holes will show if you use pins. It's also useful for securing edges for hemming and for applying trims. It is removable with water, and you can stitch through it.

Artistic Accents

Add artistic accents to your embellishment projects when you tie in fun-to-use supplies like stamps, paint, dyes, and even bleach.

DECORATIVE STITCHING

Never underestimate the creative potential of decorative stitching!

Although it's one of the easiest embellishment techniques, it can add

the same touch of visual wow as more complicated techniques.

Techniques

MACHINE MAGIC

One of the easiest ways to embellish a sewing project or purchased garment lies at your fingertips when you use your sewing machine's built-in stitches. Whether your machine features only a few decorative stitches or libraries of them, you can create a myriad of decorative effects ranging from borders and seam embellishments to elaborate designs that combine numerous stitches. You can duplicate heirloom sewing techniques with built-in heirloom stitches, drop the feed dogs for free-motion design and quilting, or use heavier threads for bobbin work.

If your machine has embroidery capabilities, you already know how much fun it is to stitch out digitized designs. But how about combining them in clever ways to take your projects beyond the ordinary? Depending on the model of your machine, specialty hoops may be available that enable you to stitch circular designs or endless borders. Other exciting software programs are available for creative monogramming techniques and digitizing your own designs. Consider projects that you can stitch entirely in the hoop or designs for faux cutwork, dimensional embroidery, and other fun effects.

EMBELLISHING WITH DECORATIVE STITCHES

Looking for a perfect way to showcase small pieces of favorite fabrics and trims and use your machine's built-in stitches? Try crazy quilting! It also provides an ideal palette for a number of other embellishments such as decorative stitches, stamping, and machine or hand embroidery. You can create it using a traditional stitch-and-flip technique on foundation cloth or paper, or step away from tradition and stitch a raw-edge contemporary crazy quilting design. Whichever technique strikes your fancy, consider using it to make quilts, jackets, throws, table runners, book covers, totes, pillows, and more. Use luxurious silk or velvet fabrics for elegant results, a mix of cotton prints and solids for casual and contemporary looks, or even plush fabrics or flannels to create an oh-so-soft baby blanket.

Traditional Crazy Quilting

You create traditional crazy quilting on a foundation fabric using a stitch-and-flip technique that allows you to create the design as you sew. The foundation fabric stabilizes the piecing and eliminates the need for paying attention to the direction of the fabric grain. You can use lightweight muslin, other lightweight cotton fabrics, or nonwoven interfacing for a lighter weight finished piece or heavier fabric like canvas where you desire extra stability.

To create a crazy quilt design:

1. Cut a piece of foundation fabric in the size desired for each block or section of your finished project, adding ½" (1.3 cm) seam allowances to all edges.

2. Cut fabric pieces with straight edges in a variety of shapes and sizes.

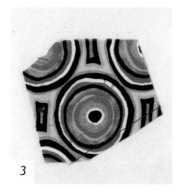
3

5

6

7

8

3. Place a piece of fabric right side up in the center of the foundation fabric and stitch along one edge.

4. Place a second piece of fabric right side down on the first piece, aligning the edges along one side. Use a ¼" (6 mm) seam allowance and stitch the edges together.

5. Press the top piece open.

6. Place a third piece of fabric right side down on the two sewn pieces, aligning the edges along one side. Stitch together using a ¼" (6 mm) seam allowance. Press the piece open.

7. Repeat to add pieces until the foundation fabric is completely covered. Trim the edges of the pieced fabrics even with the foundation fabric.

8. Use a variety of decorative stitches and assorted threads and stitch over each seam. Add additional embellishments with hand stitching, buttons, beads, or stamping as desired.

Tips: • Muslin and other cotton fabric foundations can stretch during stitching and pressing. To prevent stretching, use a dry iron for pressing and avoid pulling the fabric when stitching.

• You need longer pieces of fabric when you get to the outer edges of piecing as you sew on muslin. Cut longer pieces for this purpose or sew smaller pieces together and use as one when piecing.

• Use a variety of fabrics, mixing colors and textures to create interesting crazy quilting.

• Stabilize the wrong sides of fabrics that are very lightweight or shift easily with fusible knit interfacing before cutting and piecing.

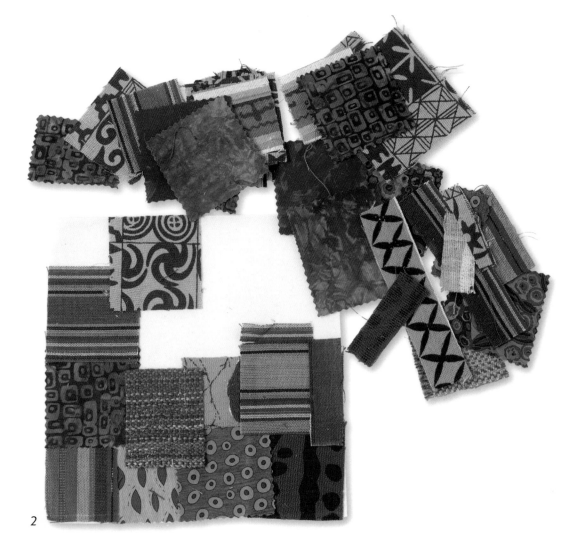

2

Raw-Edged Crazy Quilting

Have some fun and mix up traditional crazy quilting by eliminating the seams and using surface stitching to secure your patchwork design. For this technique, you will need fusible stabilizer and an assortment of fabric scraps and threads.

1. Cut a piece of stabilizer to the desired size and gather an assortment of fabric scraps in varying shapes and sizes. Trim the edges of some or all fabric pieces with pinking shears or a rotary cutter with a pinking or other decorative blade.

2. Arrange the fabric pieces on the stabilizer, overlapping the edges at least ¼" (6 mm). Make sure you have covered the stabilizer completely. Press with an iron to fuse the pieces in place.

3. Using coordinating threads and a combination of straight and decorative stitches, stitch vertical and horizontal lines across the surface until you have stitched all fabric pieces securely in place. Vary the line shapes and spacing, making some lines wavier than others and spacing some closer together and others farther apart.

4. Embellish the fabric with additional decorative stitches. If desired, hand-sew beads or buttons to the fabric or add stamped designs.

3

4

HEIRLOOM STITCHING

Many of today's sewing machines have built-in heirloom stitches that you can use for surface designs or for vintage sewing techniques such as hemstitching and fagoting.

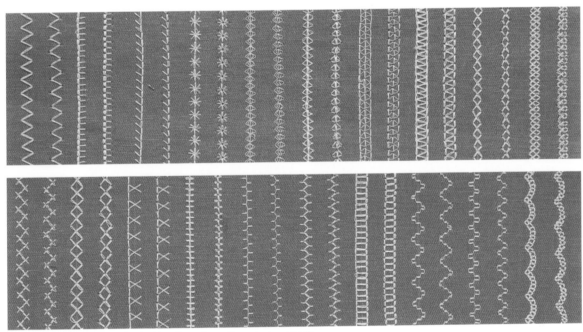

▲ Heirloom stitches stitched with universal needle and wing needle.

Hemstitching

Traditional hemstitching was hand-worked by pulling out threads parallel to a hemline, then sewing the hem in place, stitching several of the vertical threads together to create openings in the fabric. Today, you can duplicate this technique easily in a fraction of the time our grandmothers spent by using built-in machine stitches and a wing needle. It is an attractive way to secure a hem or facing on table linens or garments and is also ideal for topstitching. You can also create interesting drawn work to use for hems or surface embellishment or even to create appliqués. For best results, use light- to medium-weight linen organdy or batiste fabric.

Attaching a Hem or Facing

You can secure the edges of a hem or facing with heirloom stitches when you center them beneath the stitch. For surface designs using the same stitches, use a fabric pencil or chalk to mark a center line before stitching.

1. To attach a hem or facing with hemstitching, use a wing needle and select an heirloom stitch. If your machine doesn't have designated heirloom stitches, use a stitch that is wide and decorative such as wide zigzag stitch, daisy-chain stitch, blanket stitch, honeycomb stitch, or large cross stitch.

2. Press the hem or facing in place and pin. If desired, use a fabric marker or chalk to lightly mark the edge of the hem or facing on the right side of the fabric.

3. With the right side of the fabric up, stitch the hem or facing in place with the edge centered in the stitches.

Combining with Drawn Thread Work

You can combine some heirloom stitches with drawn thread work for interesting open effects. Use loosely woven fabric for best results.

1. For a centered open area with the stitching along the edges, pull out parallel fabric threads to make a ⅛" to ¼" (3 to 6 mm) -wide opening.

2. Select a blanket stitch. Stitch along one edge of the open area, positioning the vertical part of the stitch at the edge of the opening; the vertical stitches will bind the crosswise threads.

3. Repeat on the opposite side, starting at the same starting point to keep the stitching symmetrical.

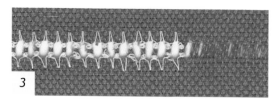

1. For stitching centered on the open work, pull out parallel threads to make two open rows, each ⅛" to ¼" (3 to 6 mm) wide with ¼" (6 mm) of fabric between the rows.

2. Select a decorative stitch such as a zigzag or cross stitch with an outline stitch along both edges. Adjust the stitch's width to span the center strip between drawn rows.

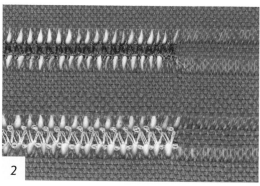

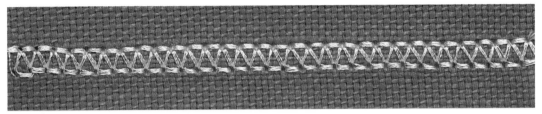

▲ Stitch used

Fagoting

Fagoting is a decorative stitch that you use to join two pieces of fabric or a piece of fabric to a trim, with a space between the joined pieces. Use 30-wt. cotton thread in the needle and bobbin thread or matching sewing thread in the bobbin.

1. Press under the fabric's edges that you wish to join. If joining to trim, press under the fabric edge only. Cut a 2" (5 cm)-wide strip of water-soluble or tear-away stabilizer that is the length of the edges to be joined. Mark two lines spaced ⅛" (3 mm) apart down the center of the stabilizer strip.

2. Baste the pieces to be joined to the stabilizer strip, aligning the edges with the marked lines.

3. Use an open toe or zigzag foot and a wide fagoting, zigzag, or any zigzag-style stitch with the width adjusted to span the opening. Stitch across the open area, making sure the needle catches the edges on both sides.

4. Remove the stabilizer.

FREE-MOTION STITCHING

With free-motion stitching, you lower the machine's feed dogs so that you can move the fabric in any direction instead of the presser foot feeding it forward or backward only. Free-motion stitching is a versatile technique, and you can use it for quilting, thread painting, and bobbin work. You can also use it to secure raw-edge appliqués or stitch layers of fabric pieces, trims, and fibers between layers of water-soluble stabilizer to create unique scarves and surface accents. Free-motion stitching is a technique that gets easier with practice; before stitching your project, practice on similar fabric to determine the design you want to stitch and achieve even stitches. You can also wear quilters' gloves for a better grip on the fabric.

1. To set up your machine for free-motion quilting or stitching, follow your machine's manual to lower the feed dogs. Attach a free-motion quilting foot, open-toe foot, or darning foot and use a new, sharp needle.

2. Hold the fabric with your fingers, positioning your hands to form a U shape with the needle. Stitch using a steady speed and move your hands smoothly to maintain even stitches. Begin and end each stitching line with several short stitches.

Consider the following types of free-motion stitching and select what works best for your project:

Outlining and Background Quilting

Stitch along the edges and details of a fabric motif for trapunto or quilting or create an allover background design to quilt a project. You can also accent fabric motifs with other colors and details or outline painted, stamped, or photo-transferred images with stitching and add details as desired.

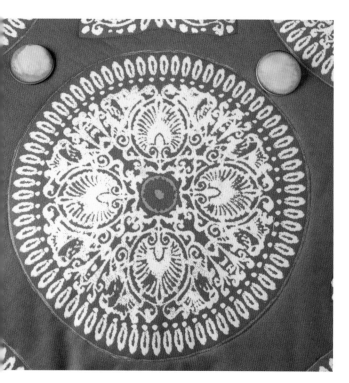

Echo Stitching

Stitch around a fabric motif, appliqué, or embroidered design; then repeat the outline in evenly spaced rows, working outward. It's especially attractive for quilting and creates a ripple effect. Use an echo-stitching foot if one is available for your machine.

1. To achieve sharp, evenly-spaced points or corners when stitching around a motif, use a fabric marker and clear ruler to draw straight lines outward from each point.

2. When stitching, drop the needle at the marked line, pivot the fabric, and continue stitching.

Stitching Layered Fabrics, Fibers, and Trims

You can use this fun technique for a variety of projects ranging from scarves to appliqués. Simply layer fabric scraps, trims, threads, or fibers between two layers of water-soluble stabilizer, making sure you connect each piece to another piece on all sides, overlapping them slightly. Stitch over the entire surface with free-motion stitching, filling in any open areas with stitches; then wash away the stabilizer.

Thread Painting

Create your own motifs by stitching an outline then stitching back and forth to create design lines and shading.

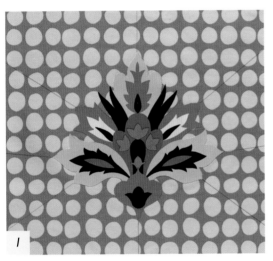

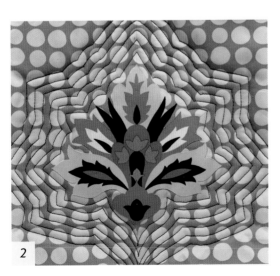

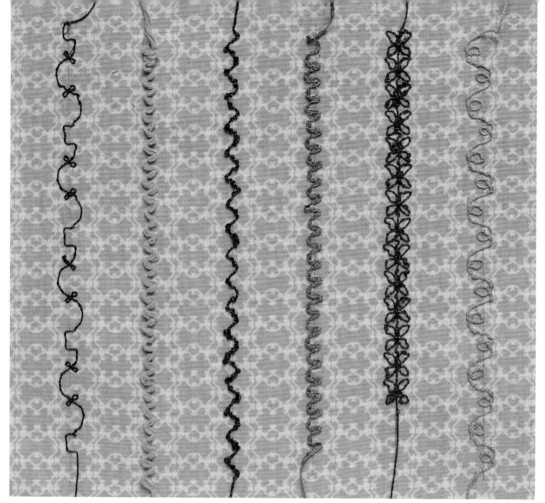

Left to right: Pearl Crown Rayon, Lightweight Yarn, Metallic Braid, Narrow Ribbon, Candlelight Metallic Yarn, Pearl Cotto

BOBBIN WORK

Bobbin work is a great way to stitch designs using threads that are too heavy for a sewing machine needle and can result in the look of hand embroidery. It is basically sewing upside down with the bobbin thread showing on the right side of the fabric. You can use your machine's utility or decorative stitches or do free-motion sewing with bobbin work.

Thread Selection

Bobbin

For the bobbin thread, you can choose from a variety of decorative threads, fine cords or braids, lightweight yarns, and narrow ribbons. For best results, use twisted threads and yarns instead of stranded threads like embroidery floss or nubby yarns that can separate or stitch unevenly.

Needle

Because the needle thread anchors the bobbin stitches in place, it will show slightly. Unless you want needle thread to stand out, use matching thread or transparent, nylon, monofilament thread.

Machine Set-up and Stitching

1. Use a needle and presser foot that are suitable for the thread and stitching technique. The feed dogs should remain up unless you are doing free-motion stitching.

2. Some machines come with a separate bobbin case that's configured for bobbin work; if yours doesn't, you may want to purchase one for bobbin work to avoid having to readjust the tension for regular stitching. If the thread is fine enough, you can wind it slowly on the machine, making sure it winds evenly and does not fill past the edge of the bobbin. Otherwise, hand-wind the bobbin smoothly and evenly.

3. Tension is the most important adjustment when it comes to bobbin work. If your machine has a special bobbin-work bobbin, follow your machine's manual to set it up. Otherwise, you will need either to loosen or bypass the bobbin case tension; experiment until you achieve neat, even stitches.

4. It's fun to experiment with different stitches for bobbin work. Some work better than others, especially with heavier-weight threads, yarns, and cords. In general, more airy, open stitches stitch out better than tight stitching, and you can achieve interesting results with just a basic straight stitch. Whenever possible, select a longer stitch length and wider width, although you may not have this option for some decorative stitches.

5. Because you are stitching with the wrong side of the fabric up and will want to stabilize the fabric, an easy way to mark a design for stitching is on the paper side of the fusible stabilizer; after marking, fuse the stabilizer to the wrong side of the fabric.

6. To begin stitching, rotate the handwheel on your machine to pull the bobbin thread through the stitch plate. Pull approximately 3" (7.6 cm) of both threads to the back of the presser foot. Place stabilizer on the wrong side of the fabric and place the fabric right side down to stitch. Hold the bobbin thread tail out of the way and stitch. Leave a tail several inches long at the end of the stitching. Use a tapestry needle to pull the thread ends to the wrong side of the fabric and knot.

Note: Test-stitch on a scrap of the fabric you're using before starting your project. The bobbin thread should be smooth and flat on the surface of the fabric; adjust the tension or the stitch length if needed.

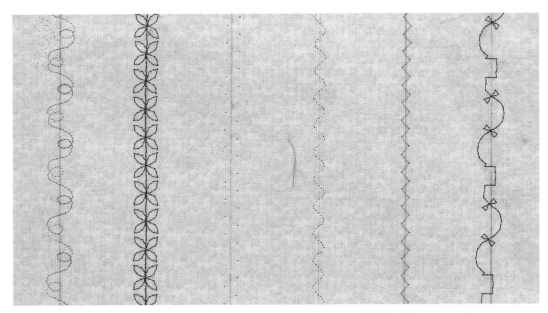

▲ Mark lines or designs for stitching on stabilizer; needle threads shown are Polylite, all-purpose sewing and clear monofilament.

DIGITIZED MACHINE EMBROIDERY

If your sewing machine has digitized-embroidery capabilities, you most likely know how to embroider basic digitized designs. But why not take your machine embroidery a step further and have fun with appliqué, cutwork, dimensional designs, monogramming, and projects worked in the hoop.

Appliqué Embroidery Designs

These designs are specifically digitized to create an embroidered appliqué on fabric. See the list of sources (page 142).

1. Load the appliqué embroidery design into your machine. Hoop the fabric with stabilizer on the wrong side.

2. Stitch the first color stop; this first programmed stitch of the appliqué design will be an outline. After the machine stitches the outline, cut a piece of fabric slightly larger than the outline.

3. Place the fabric over the stitched outline and stitch the second color stop. This stitch will tack the fabric in place with the same outline. Remove the hoop from the machine but do not remove the fabric from the hoop. Using small, sharp scissors, trim the appliqué fabric close to the stitching.

4. Replace the hoop on the machine. Complete embroidering the design. When the machine has finished the embroidery, remove the hoop from the machine and the fabric from the hoop. Remove the stabilizer.

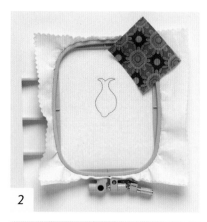

2

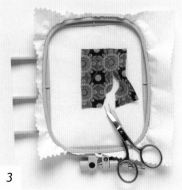

3

4

Free-standing Embroidered Appliqués

You can use any digitized embroidery design to create a free-standing appliqué. These appliqués are especially useful when you want to add an embroidered design to an area of a garment or accessory that would be difficult to hoop and embroider. They are also a great way to add embroidered designs to fabrics that are too thick for embroidery or to nonfabric objects like canvas, baskets, or frames. You can sew or glue the appliqué flat onto the surface or leave the edges free.

1. Load the embroidery design into your machine. Use felt for a heavier-weight appliqué or tear-away or water-soluble stabilizer for a lighter-weight appliqué.

2. Hoop the fabric or stabilizer and embroider the design. Remove the fabric from the hoop. Remove the stabilizer or use small sharp scissors to trim the fabric close to the stitching.

3. Sew or glue the appliqué to the surface of your choice.

Dimensional Designs and Appliqués

Dimensional machine–embroidery designs range from free-standing projects to designs with fringed accents or padding. Use them for decorations or to accent pillows, tote bags, and other accessories. You can also create your own dimensional designs by embroidering a design on nonfraying fabric like felt or faux suede and then cutting it out close to the stitching.

Although the steps will vary slightly for each design, the following is an example of how to make a free-standing flower using a digitized 3D design on organza or linen fabric:

1. Load the embroidery design file into your machine.

2. Hoop the fabric with clear, wash-away stabilizer on the wrong side. Embroider the top layer of the flower including the petals and center outline with placement mark. Remove the fabric from the hoop. Using small, sharp scissors, trim close to the embroidered design. Remove the stabilizer or leave it in for more body. If your design has several layers, repeat this step for all layers except the bottom.

3. For the bottom layer, hoop another piece of fabric with wash-away stabilizer on the wrong side. Embroider the bottom layer including the petals and center outline with placement mark. Leave the fabric in the hoop and the hoop in the machine. Use a small amount of spray adhesive and adhere the center of the top layer to the center of the bottom layer, aligning the center outlines and placement marks. Allow the adhesive to dry.

4. Resume the color stop order and embroider the flower center.

5. Remove the fabric from the hoop. Trim the fabric close to the bottom layer of the flower.

Cutwork

Cutwork has never been so easy! Thanks to machine-embroidery designs that are digitized to create faux cutwork, you can create elegant looks on linens, garments, and accessories in a fraction of the time it takes to stitch traditional cutwork. Use tone-on-tone thread and fabric colors for a classic look or give your designs a contemporary edge by using contrasting colors. For best results, use closely-woven linen or cotton fabrics.

1. Load an embroidery cutwork design into your machine. Use light- to medium-weight natural-fiber fabric such as cotton or linen with a tight weave.

2. Hoop the fabric with a fabric-like water-soluble stabilizer on the wrong side.

3. Stitch the first color stop to outline the cutout areas. Remove the hoop from the machine but do not remove the fabric from the hoop. Use small sharp scissors to cut out the fabric close to the stitching in the outlined areas, being careful not to cut the stabilizer.

4. Replace the hoop in the machine and finish embroidering the design. The machine will stitch the bars of the cutwork onto the stabilizer.

5. Remove the fabric from the hoop. Trim any excess stabilizer with scissors; then hold the fabric under warm water to dissolve the remaining stabilizer. Place it flat on a towel and blot excess moisture. Press while still slightly damp to prevent wrinkling.

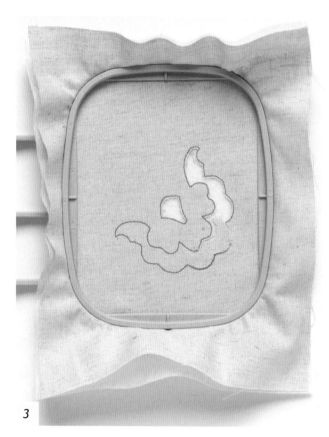

Faux cutwork has the look of cutwork but doesn't actually have any cutout areas. It is ideal for many of the same uses as regular cutwork.

Monogramming

Always popular, monogramming is easy to do with any sewing machine that has a built-in alphabet with a choice of layouts and fonts. You can expand your options even more with digitized machine-embroidery designs that often include unique fonts, borders, and background details. The following are guidelines for traditional monogram layouts, but really, almost anything goes; experiment with fonts and layouts that you like and use the one that best suits your project.

- A traditional woman's monogram features a large initial for her last name in the center with the initial for her first name on the left and the initial for her middle or maiden name on the right.

- A traditional man's monogram features three same-size letters with first, middle, and last initial in that order.

- A traditional couple's monogram features a larger last initial in the center with the woman's first initial on the left and the man's first initial on the right.

You can also purchase custom monogramming software that makes it easy to create beautiful monograms in assorted layouts, combined with borders, frames, other embroidered designs, and appliqués. With these programs, you can design the monogram on your computer and then transfer it to your machine for stitching. These programs allow you to change colors and sizes and combine motifs. Depending on the program, it may also show the stitching order and a 3-D view of the design.

Tablet Cover

Protect your e-tablet and carry it in style when you make a sturdy cover. You piece the outside with traditional crazy quilting, and the inside features elastic corners to securely hold the tablet in place.

MATERIALS

Fabrics

Assorted fabrics, cut into large strips and rectangles for piecing four 4" (10.2 cm) squares with machine-embroidered motifs

¼ yd (0.2 m) of 44" (111.8 cm)-wide duck canvas as the foundation fabric

¼ yd (0.2 m) of coordinating fabric for lining

¼ yd (0.2 m) of coordinating fabric for binding

Other Supplies

⅓ yd (0.3 m) of 20" (50.8 cm)-wide, one-sided, fusible, ultra-firm stabilizer

⅓ yd (0.3 m) of 20" (50.8 cm)-wide, fusible, featherweight interfacing

two 7¾" × 9¾" (19.7 × 24.8 cm) rectangles of poster board or purchased tablet shapers

¼ yd (0.2 m) of ⅜" (9 mm)-wide, coordinating, grosgrain ribbon

½ yd (0.5 m) of ¼" (6 mm)-wide elastic

¼" (6 mm)-wide, double-stick, fusible web tape

elastic ponytail holder and two ½" to ¾" (1.3 to 1.9 cm)-diameter buttons with shanks for closure

threads: all-purpose, 30-wt. cotton, metallic, and 40-wt. machine-embroidery rayon

embellishments of your choice, such as buttons or beads

Finished Size

8½" × 10¾" (21.6 × 27.3 cm)

Cutting

1. From the canvas fabric, cut two 9" × 10¾" (22.9 × 27.3 cm) rectangles.

2. From the lining fabric, fusible stabilizer, and fusible interfacing, cut one 10¾" × 17" (27.3 × 43.2 cm) rectangle each.

3. From the binding fabric, cut and piece a 2½" × 60" (6.4 × 152.4 cm) strip.

2

Assembly

Note: Use a ¼" (6 mm) seam allowance and sew seams with right sides together unless otherwise indicated.

1. Follow the instructions for traditional crazy quilting (page 20) to crazy quilt the two canvas rectangles, including two machine-embroidered squares on each panel. Sew the panels together along one long edge, using a ½" (1.3 cm) seam allowance. Press the seam open.

2. Using the built-in decorative stitches on your sewing machine, stitch over each piecing seam and the seam joining the panels. Also use decorative stitches to create allover designs or rows of decorative stitches across the fabric pieces. Add buttons or beads as desired.

3. Follow the manufacturer's instructions to fuse the stabilizer to the wrong side of the crazy quilt panel and the interfacing to the wrong side of the lining panel.

4. To add elastic for securing your e-tablet to the lining, press the lining rectangle in half crosswise with wrong sides together. With the right half on top, make marks on the side and on the top and bottom edges, 3" (76 mm) from each corner. Cut the elastic into four equal lengths. Open the lining rectangle and sew the elastic to the lining at the marks, keeping the elastic taut.

5. With wrong sides together, stitch the outer panel to the lining panel ⅛" (3 mm) from the side and bottom edges. Place a strip of fusible-web tape on the wrong side of the ribbon and adhere it to the center of the lining panel. Stitch along both edges of the ribbon. Insert the poster board or tablet-shaper rectangles between the lining and outer panels on each side of the center ribbon.

6. Press the binding strip in half lengthwise with wrong sides together. Open the strip and press the long edges under to meet at the center fold. Press in half again. Apply fusible web tape along the long edges of the binding strip. Removing the paper backing as you go, wrap the binding around the edges of the cover, mitering the corners. Fuse in place.

7. From the outer cover side, edge-stitch the binding in place, making sure the edge on the lining side is caught in the stitching.

8. To create the closure, sew a button with a shank to the center of each short edge, 1" (2.5 cm) from the edge. Wrap the ponytail holder over the buttons to secure. Tack or glue the ponytail holder in place under the button on the back of the cover.

4

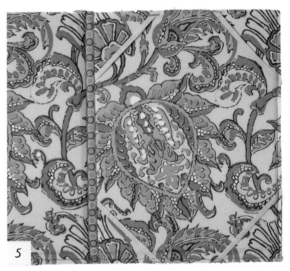

5

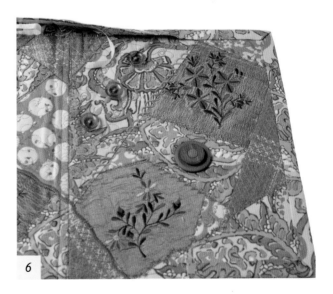

6

Globe-trotting Tote

Because the piecing involves no seams, contemporary crazy quilting is an ideal technique to use with handwoven and other heavier-weight fabrics. This tote features a combination of richly textured woven silk, handwoven African cottons, colorful Polynesian batiks, and fun quilting-cotton prints. Hand-rolled paper beads carry out the global theme and assorted buttons provide the finishing touches.

MATERIALS

Fabrics

assorted fabrics, cut into squares and rectangles ranging from 1½"–3" (3.8 –7.6 cm) wide and 2" to 5" (5 to 12.7 cm) long for piecing

½ yd (0.5 m) of coordinating fabric for the lining

¼ yd (0.2 m) of coordinating fabric for handles

Other Supplies

one yd (0.9 m) of 18" (45.7 cm)-wide, fusible stabilizer

¾ yd (0.7 m) of 44" (111.8 cm)-wide, fusible fleece

threads: all-purpose, variegated cotton and polyester, machine-embroidery rayon

embellishments of your choice, such as buttons, beads, yarns for machine couching, or bead strings for hand-couching.

Finished Size

11" × 14" × 3" (27.9 × 35.6 × 76 mm)

Cutting

1. From the fusible stabilizer and fusible fleece, cut two 15½" × 16½" (39.4 × 41.9 cm) rectangles each. Also cut two 5" × 22" (12.7 × 55.9 cm) strips from the fleece.

2. From the lining fabric, cut two 15½" × 16½" (39.4 × 41.9 cm) rectangles.

3. From the handle fabric, cut two 5" × 22" (12.7 × 55.9 cm) strips.

Assembly

Note: Use a ½" (1.3 cm) seam allowance and sew seams with right sides together.

1. Follow the instructions for raw-edged crazy quilting (page 22) to crazy-quilt and embellish the two rectangles of stabilizer. Follow the manufacturer's instructions to fuse a fleece rectangle to the wrong side of each crazy-quilt rectangle.

2. With the right sides together, sew the embellished panels along the side and bottom edges. Press the seams open. To create the bottom of the bag fold each corner with the bottom and side seams aligned and centered. Draw a 3" (7.6 cm)-long line across the point, then stitch on the line. Trim the excess fabric. Turn the bag right side out and press.

3. To make each handle, fuse a fleece strip to the wrong side of the handle strip. Press in half with wrong sides together. Open the strip and press the long edges under to meet at the center fold. Press in half again. Topstitch close to both long edges.

4. With raw edges even, baste the handle ends to the top edge of the bag, 3½" (8.9 cm) from the side seams.

5. Sew the side and bottom edges of the lining rectangles together, leaving an 8" (20.3 cm) opening in the bottom seam for turning. Follow Step 2 to shape the bottom corners of the lining. Press, but do not turn right side out.

6. Insert the bag in the lining with right sides together, aligning the side seams and top edges. Sew the top edges together.

7. Pull the bag through the opening in the lining, turning the lining right side out. Stitch the opening in the lining closed. Insert the lining in the bag and press the top edge. Topstitch ½" (1.3 cm) from the edge.

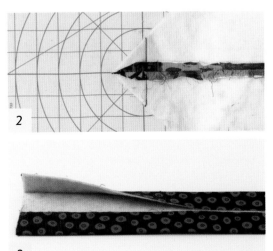

2

3

7

Monogrammed Table Topper

Combine specialty feet and attachments, monogramming, decorative stitches, and ribbon to make a personalized table topper with purchased napkins and wool felt. Because the napkin edges are already finished, you can simply join them together and trim them; you can also substitute 1¼ yards (1.1 m) of cotton or linen fabric and hem the edges.

MATERIALS

Fabrics

18" (45.7 cm) square of wool felt for center

4" × 6" (10.2 × 15.2 cm) scrap of fabric for monogram appliqué

four 20" (50.8 cm)-square, cloth napkins or 1¼ yd (1.1 m) of fabric

¾ yd (0.7 m) of 58" (147.3 cm)-wide, coordinating linen for border

4½ yd (4.1 m) of ⅜" (1 cm)-wide, grosgrain ribbon

Other Supplies

four chair ties with tassels

permanent fabric adhesive

stabilizer: tear-away and wash-away

digitized machine embroidery designs: appliqué monogram letter, approximately 3½ "(8.9 cm) high and flower, approximately 1" (2.5 cm) high

threads: all-purpose, 12- and 30-wt. cotton and 40-wt. machine-embroidery rayon

edge-joining machine foot (optional)

circle template or circular sewing attachment (optional)

monogramming software (optional)

Finished Size

50" × 50" (127 × 127 cm)

Embroidered Center Panel

1. If you're using monogramming software, plan your design with a center monogram and eight flowers arranged in a circle around it. The diameter of the combined motifs is 6¼" (15.9 cm). Save the design and transfer it to your machine. Otherwise, load the designs into your machine and plan to stitch them in the same arrangement given.

2. Hoop the center of the felt square with the stabilizer underneath. Refer to the instructions for the appliqué embroidery and embroider the designs using rayon thread. Use built-in machine stitches and randomly stitch eyelet stitches around the embroidered motifs.

3. Mark the center of the embroidered design with a pin. Measuring out from the center, use a disappearing, fine-tip fabric marker and a circle template to draw a circle with a 3¾" (9.5 cm) radius from the center. Repeat to draw circles radiating outward at ½" to ¾" (1.3 to 1.9 cm) intervals until you reach a circle with a 5½" (14 cm) radius from the center.

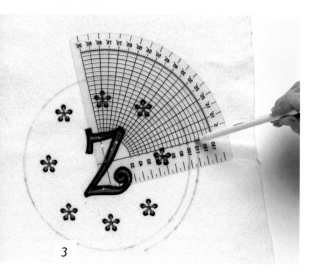

3

4. Use built-in machine stitches to stitch along the lines. If desired, use a circular attachment on your machine to easily stitch circular rows of decorative stitches. Trim the felt in a circle ½" (1.3 cm) from the outside row of stitching.

Topper Piecing

1. For the borders, cut four 6½" × 50" (16.5 × 127 cm) strips. If you aren't using purchased napkins, cut four 21" (53.3 cm) squares from the fabric. Hem each square with a ½" (1.3 cm) hem.

2

2. Place two napkins or hemmed squares side-by-side with ends even and stitch them together using a 3-step zigzag stitch and an edge-joining foot. If you don't have an edge-joining foot, use a regular foot and stitch carefully, keeping the edges side by side without overlapping or leaving a space. Repeat to join the two remaining napkins; then join the two sets of napkins together to make a square.

3. Cut the ribbon in half lengthwise. With the ribbon end extending 1" (2.5 cm) beyond the topper edge, center one ribbon strip over a joined seam and edge-stitch it in place along both long edges. Trim 1" (2.5 cm) past the opposite topper edge. Repeat to sew the ribbon across the remaining seam. Press the ends to the wrong side and slip-stitch in place.

4. For each border strip, press under a doubled ½" (1.3 cm) hem on one long edge. Mark the center of the hemmed edge on each border strip. Mark the center of each edge of the topper. Matching the marks for the centers, refer to instructions for fagoting (page 25) and attach the borders to the topper with a fagoting, double cross stitch. Stop stitching at each of the topper corners.

5. To miter each border corner, fold the topper in half diagonally with right sides together and edges even. Draw a 45-degree angle from the topper corner to the outer edge of the border strips. Stitch along the line; then trim the excess fabric. Press the seams open.

6. Press the border edges under in a doubled ½" (1.3 cm) hem. Refer to the instructions for hemstitching (page 23) to secure the hem with a large cross stitch.

7. Apply fusible web to the wrong side of the embroidered felt circle, trimming the web edges even with the circle. Remove the paper backing and fuse the circle to the center of the topper. Edge-stitch it in place.

8. For each chair tie, place the tassels side by side and tie the cord into an overhand knot 1" (2.5 cm) above the top of the tassels. Press the knot as flat as you can with a warm iron. Apply permanent fabric adhesive to the back of the knot, cut the cord ends and press them into the adhesive to secure. Glue the knotted tassels to each topper corner, placing the knot 1" (2.5 cm) above the edge.

APPLIQUÉ

  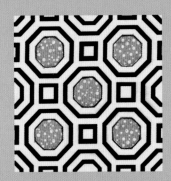

Like many embellishment techniques, appliqué offers unlimited
options for creativity. You can finish edges, leave them raw, create
reverse looks, make borders, combine them with free-motion quilting,
machine embroidery, and other decorative stitches...and so much more.
They're also the perfect canvas for decorative threads and trims.

Techniques

DESIGN SELECTION

Many commercial appliqué patterns and books are available in fabric and quilt shops to use as starting points, but it's easy to design your own. If you're an artist, you can translate almost anything you can draw to an appliqué design. And don't worry if you aren't, you can create your own designs in other ways. An easy way to design is to use individual fabric motifs or a combination of motifs. Fabric motifs offer a world of potential for appliqués; used alone or combined, they are ideal for creating borders, raw-edge designs, and collages. Are you a photographer? You don't have to be a professional to take a photograph of your favorite pet, a beautiful flower, or a gorgeous sunset and use it to create an appliqué design. Also consider drawing inspiration from nature; a walk outdoors can result in discovering leaves and flowers that you can use for interesting designs.

FABRIC SELECTION

Good-quality cotton prints and solids are always go-to fabrics for appliqué. Available in an almost endless variety of prints, styles, and colors, you can use them for a wide variety of finished and raw edge techniques. Large motifs are ideal for cutting out and using as stitched or dimensional appliqués, and you can also create a collage of fabric pieces or strips and cut appliqués from the collage. Lightweight tweed, wool, or linen fabrics can add textures to designs and provide interesting raw edges. And for reverse appliqué, raw-edge appliqués that don't fray, and dimensional appliqués, you can't beat wool felt, faux suede, or leather and other nonwoven fabrics.

Appliqué Preparation

You prepare an appliqué motif in several ways for stitching, and the best one to use depends on the finished look you want as well as your personal preferences. Remember to reverse the pattern when tracing it onto the wrong side of the fabric.

Plastic Template

You can make templates of your appliqué motifs with sturdy template plastic, and these templates are a good idea if you will be cutting out multiple pieces of the same shape.

1. Use a permanent marker and trace the outline of your motif pattern onto the plastic. Cut out the template using a craft knife.

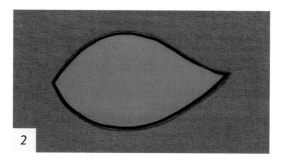

2

2. Place the template on the wrong side of the fabric and trace around the edges. Cut the fabric out on the marked line.

3. Pin or baste the appliqué to the background fabric.

Freezer Paper Template

Temporary templates that you make with freezer paper or self-adhesive, fabric-like, water-soluble stabilizer are useful if you want to press under the edges of the appliqué before stitching.

1. Draw the motif on the dull side of freezer paper or the fabric side of the stabilizer and cut it out.

2. For paper, place the shiny side on the wrong side of the fabric and press it in place. For stabilizer, remove the paper backing and adhere the template to the wrong side of the fabric. Leave at least ½" (1.3 cm) between the pieces if cutting out multiple pieces. Cut the fabric out ³⁄₁₆" to ¼"(5 to 6 mm) beyond the edge.

3. Use small, sharp scissors to clip the extending fabric to the template along curves and at corners. Use the tip of a dry iron to press the fabric over the edge of the freezer paper.

4. When the edges have cooled, remove the freezer paper. You can also remove it after stitching by cutting a small slit in the background fabric under the appliqué and pulling out the paper.

5. Pin or baste the appliqué to the background fabric.

Fusible Web Backing

Fusible web with paper backing on both sides is a quick, easy way to prepare an appliqué.

1. Check to see which side of the paper backing is easiest to remove and trace the pattern onto the other sheet. Cut the pattern out at least ¼" (6 mm) from the outline.

2. Remove the unmarked paper backing and place the motif web side down on the wrong side of the fabric. Cut the appliqué out along the outline.

3. Remove the paper backing and position the appliqué on the background fabric. Press it with a warm iron to fuse in place.

2

3

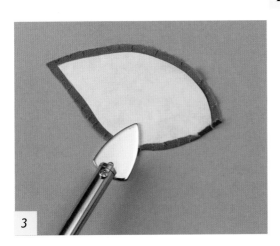

Stabilizer Sheets

Printable, self-adhesive, water-soluble stabilizer sheets are ideal if you want to use a photograph or computer-generated design to make appliqués. You can also use the copy feature of your printer to print the design. Because the stabilizer is on the right side of the fabric, you can also see the detail lines for free-motion stitching or other embellishment.

1. Use an ink-jet printer to print the photograph or design from your computer onto the fabric side of the stabilizer sheet. This method also gives you the opportunity to be creative with photo editing software as shown in the second photo. Or use the copy feature of your printer to copy a design onto the fabric side.

2. If you are using a photograph for your appliqué design, use a fine-tip permanent marker to outline the main design lines of the photograph that will be cut from different fabrics. You can add details later with stitching. If your photograph has a foreground and background like the photo shown, print a second sheet and cut the background (sky in sample) from one sheet and the foreground objects (trees in sample) from the second sheet.

3. Cut out the pieces. Remove the paper backing and smooth the stabilizer piece onto the right side of the fabric.
Note: The photograph will not be reversed when finished. Cut out the fabric pieces.

4. Use temporary basting spray or a fabric glue stick to apply the pieces to the background fabric. Stitch the edges in place with satin or straight edges. If your photograph has a pieced background with foreground appliqués like the photo shown, stitch the edges of the background pieces before adhering it to the foreground pieces.

5. Set your machine for free-motion stitching and add detail lines to the design. When you have completed the stitching, use small sharp scissors to carefully cut away as much stabilizer as possible without cutting the stitches. Remove any remaining stabilizer by submerging the piece in water for two to three minutes and gently rubbing the stabilizer until it dissolves. Air-dry it on a towel.

FINISHED EDGE APPLIQUÉ

Finished edges are suitable for a wide variety of appliquéd projects. A finished edge will not ravel and is more durable than a raw edge for items that people will wear or launder. The best stitching technique to use depends on the look you want. Satin stitches are a good choice for almost any fabric or design, and you can set the stitch width and length to achieve the desired density. You can also use decorative stitches that are wide enough to secure the edges. If you turned under the appliqué edges during preparation, you can stitch along the edges or use a blanket stitch or other decorative stitch without the edges fraying.

Satin Stches

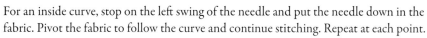

Set your machine for a short zigzag stitch or similar decorative stitch in a width that is proportionate to the size of the appliqué piece. Position your fabric under the needle so that the left swing of the needle is on the appliqué fabric and the right swing is on the foundation fabric, just past the edge of the appliqué. Bring the bobbin thread to the surface of the fabric and begin stitching in the center of an edge, not at a corner. For best results, stitch slowly at an even pace.

Corners

To turn corners without leaving a gap in the stitching, put the needle down in the fabric just past the corner, pivot, and continue stitching.

Curves

Smooth pivoting at regular intervals is the key to success when it comes to stitching curves. To ensure smooth stitching, use a disappearing fabric pencil and mark evenly-spaced pivot points along the curve or mentally picture these points as you stitch. Plan to pivot more often on a gradual curve than on a sharp curve.

For an inside curve, stop on the left swing of the needle and put the needle down in the fabric. Pivot the fabric to follow the curve and continue stitching. Repeat at each point.

For an outside curve, at the first point, stop on the right swing of the needle and put the needle down in the fabric. Pivot the fabric to follow the curve and continue stitching. Repeat at each point.

Perfect points

Stitching points is a little trickier than corners or curves because it's necessary to adjust the stitch width to fit the point.

To stitch a perfect inside point, use a fabric pencil to lightly draw guidelines equal to the stitch width to help you maintain a consistent width. Stitch slowly past the point until the swing of the needle touches the guideline of the second edge and stop with the needle down in the fabric.

Gradually decrease the stitch width until you reach zero at the point. Stop at the point with the needle down, pivot the fabric and begin increasing the stitch width as you stitch the second edge.

To stitch outside points, stitch slowly as you approach the point until the swing of the needle touches the opposite side of the point. Stop with the needle down in the fabric. Decrease the stitch width until you reach zero at the point. Lift the presser foot, pivot the fabric, and begin increasing the stitch width as you stitch away from the point.

RAW-EDGE APPLIQUÉ

This technique is quick and easy and results in a more unstructured, casual look than stitched-edge appliqué designs, especially when you use woven fabrics. You can fuse the appliqués in place and stitch closely to or overcast the edge for slight fraying or create a more frayed edge by not fusing the edges. Raw edge appliqués provide a great canvas for free-motion stitching and other embellishment details. For an edge that doesn't fray at all, use nonwoven fabrics like felt or faux suede.

1. Cut the appliqué motif from fabric. With the motif right side up, trace the outline onto the paper backing of the fusible web. To fuse the entire motif, cut the shape from the fusible web. To leave the edges unfused and cut it out ¼" (6 mm) inside the traced line. Fuse it to the wrong side of the appliqué.

2. Remove the paper backing and fuse the appliqué in place. If you want only to tack the center of the appliqué to the background fabric, use a small circle of fusible web or fabric adhesive or temporary basting spray to secure it for stitching. *Note:* Use a press cloth if applying faux suede.

3. Stitch the motif in place ⅛" to ¼" (3 to 6 mm) from the edge, using a straight stitch, zigzag stitch, blanket stitch, or other decorative stitch.

4. Stitch detail lines as desired, using free-motion or regular stitches.

DIMENSIONAL APPLIQUÉ

Dimensional appliqués add a touch of fun to your projects and can have raw or finished edges. Attach them to the background fabric with stitching, couched trims, or buttons or beads.

Raw Edge

1. Fabrics like felt or faux suede are naturals for raw-edge dimensional appliqués. Trace the appliqué design onto the wrong side of the fabric; then cut them out. Embellish with stitching, trims, or other details. Stitch them in place with couched trims or center stitches.

2. You can also use woven fabrics and motifs to create dimensional appliqués. For each appliqué, fuse the wrong sides of two pieces of fabric together with fusible web. Trace the appliqué design onto one side of the fabric and cut it out. To use a fabric motif, cut out a piece of fabric with the motif centered. Cut a piece of backing fabric the same size and fuse the wrong sides together. Cut out the motif. Stitch the edges and details with regular or free-motion stitching.

Finished Edge

You make finished-edge dimensional appliqués by sewing two pieces of fabric together. For lightweight fabrics, apply fusible, featherweight interfacing to the wrong side of the appliqué before cutting it out.

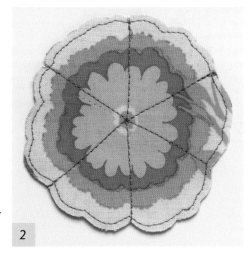

1. To use a pattern, trace the appliqué motif onto the wrong side of one fabric piece. Layer the fabric pieces with right sides together and stitch along the marked line. Cut the appliqué out ⅛" (3 mm) from the stitching line.

2. To use a fabric motif, cut the motif out, adding a ¼" (6 mm) seam allowance. Cut a piece of fabric the same size for the back. With right sides together, sew the motif to the backing fabric using a ¼" (6 mm) seam allowance. Trim the seam allowance to ⅛" (3 mm). Cut a slit in the center of the back fabric for turning.

3. Turn right side out and press. Slip-stitch the opening edges closed. Topstitch close to the edge of the appliqué.

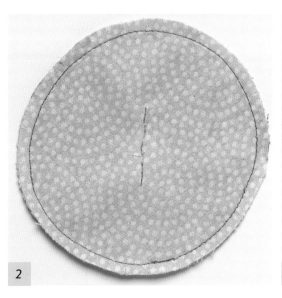

REVERSE APPLIQUÉ

In contrast to other techniques where you apply appliqués to the surface of the background fabric, for reverse appliqué you layer the background fabric on top of one or more appliqué fabrics. The shape is cut from the background fabric, revealing the fabric underneath. Experiment with fabric combinations and with cutting appliqués that showcase multiple layers of fabric.

Finish the edges of cutout areas on woven fabrics with satin stitches, decorative stitches, or couched trims. It isn't necessary to finish the edges of nonfraying fabrics like felt or suede.

Basic Reverse Appliqué

1. Use a fabric marker or chalk pencil to draw the outline of the reverse appliqué onto the background fabric or onto a surface appliqué as shown in the sample. Or mark areas of the fabric motifs to be cut out.

2. Cut a piece of fabric for the appliqué that is at least 1" (2.5 cm) larger than the appliqué outline. With the fabrics right side up, pin or baste the appliqué fabric to the wrong side of the background fabric behind the area to be cut out. Straight stitch on the marked appliqué outline. Remove the pins or basting stitches. Use small, sharp scissors to carefully cut the top layer of fabric out of the stitched area.

3. If desired, add one or more additional reverse appliqués to the reverse appliqué. Mark the area to be cut out and repeat Step 2. Repeat for each layer of fabric.

4. Finish the edges as desired.

1

2

3

Fused Reverse Appliqué

Because you fuse the edges for this technique, stitching around the cutout area is optional. It is a good choice for one or more details on a surface appliqué that you will fuse in place.

1. Draw the area or areas to be cut out on the surface appliqué. Trace the outline of the surface appliqué with the reverse appliqué's outline onto the paper backing of two sheets of double stick fusible web. Cut out ½" (1.3 cm) from the surface appliqué outline on both sheets.

2

2. Fuse one surface-appliqué pattern to the wrong side of the surface-appliqué fabric. Cut out along the outline. Cut out the opening(s) for the reverse appliqué(s).

3. Fuse the remaining appliqué pattern to the wrong side of the reverse appliqué fabric. Cut out the reverse appliqué ½" (1.3 cm) from the outline(s).

4. Remove the paper backing from the surface appliqué. Center the reverse appliqué right side down over the wrong side of the cutout area and finger press in place.

5. Turn the piece right side up and press it in place on the background fabric. Stitch the appliqué and cutout edges in place as desired.

4

5

Appliquéd Chair Cushion

You will be sitting pretty when you make this comfy cushion with fun appliqués and whimsical trims. It's also easy to adapt the design to cushions or pillows of any size. Simply repeat the motifs in other fabrics as many times as you like.

MATERIALS

Fabrics

⅞ yd (0.8 m) of 44" (111.8 cm)- or 54" (137.2 cm)-wide print decorator fabric for cushion piecing, back, and ties

¼ yd (0.2 m) of 54" (137.2 cm)-wide solid color decorator fabric without nap for top piecing or ⅝ yd (0.6 m) for fabric with nap

large scraps of coordinating print and solid fabrics for appliqués

2¼" (5.7 cm) -diameter circle of faux suede for flower center

½ yd (0.5 m) of 2" (5 cm)-wide double-sided satin ribbon for flower center

Other Supplies

three ½" (1.3 cm)-square buttons for flower center

one yd (0.9 m) each of ¼" (6 mm)-wide decorative trim, ⅛" (3 mm)-diameter twisted cord and ¼" (6 mm)-wide ribbon

three 9" × 12" (22.9 × 30.5 cm) sheets of double-sided fusible web

¼" (6 mm)-wide double-sided fusible web tape

20" × 20" (50.8 × 50.8 cm)-square of fusible featherweight interfacing

two ⅞" (2.2 cm)-diameter cover buttons

polyester fiberfill

all-purpose thread

waxed button thread

6" (15.2 cm)-long upholstery needle

Specialty Presser Feet

cording or beads and pearls foot
adjustable zipper foot

Finished Size

17" × 17" × 2" (43.2 × 43.2 × 5 cm)

Cutting and Piecing Top

Note: Use a ½" (1.3 cm) seam allowance and sew seams with right sides together.

1. From the print decorator fabric, cut two 4" × 20" (10.2 × 50.8 cm) strips and one 6" × 20" (15.2 × 50.8 cm) strip for the top piecing, one 20" × 20" (50.8 × 50.8 cm) square for the back, and two 4" × 22" (10.2 × 55.9 cm) strips for the ties.

2. From the solid decorator fabric, cut four 3" × 20" (7.6 × 50.8 cm) strips.

3. Refer to the photograph on page 54 and sew the solid and print decorator-fabric strips together, beginning and ending with solid-color strips and placing the 6" (15.2 cm)-wide print strip in the center. Press the seams. Trim each back corner into a curve.

Appliqués

1. Following the instructions for fused appliqué (page 49), trace the Flower A pattern (page 58) and four center motif patterns onto the fusible-web paper backing and fuse it to the wrong side of the appropriate fabrics. Remove the paper backing from the center motifs and fuse them to the center of the flower.

2. Following the instructions for fused reverse appliqué on page 53, trace two complete Flower B/C patterns onto the fusible web paper backing. Fuse the complete patterns to the wrong side of the flower and flower center fabrics. Carefully cut the fabric for the center out of the flower fabric and set it aside to use for Flower C. Trim the center fabric ½" (1.3 cm) beyond the center outline.

3. Remove the paper backing from Flower B and adhere the center appliqué fabric to the wrong side.

4. Apply fusible-web tape to the wrong side of the ¼" (6 mm)-wide ribbon.

5. Remove the paper backing from the remaining appliqués and ribbon. Refer to the photo and position the appliqués on the pieced cushion top with the edges at least 1½"–2" (3.8–5 cm) from the cushion edge. Cut and arrange the ribbon as desired, inserting the ends under the appliqué edges or placing them at the cushion edges.

6. Finish the edges of the appliqués with satin stitches (page 49), decorative stitches (page 23), couched cording (page 72), flat trim (page 75), or edge-stitched trim as desired. Sew the ribbon vine in place with a long, wide, zigzag stitch.

7. To embellish the Flower A center, refer to the instructions for the gathered flower center (page 75). For the Flower C center, cut ½" (1.3 cm)-long

slits in the edge of the faux suede circle. Use a small piece of fusible web and a press cloth to adhere the center to the flower. Hand-sew three small buttons in the center.

Assembly

1. For the ties, fold each strip in half lengthwise with right sides together. Sew the raw edges together, stitching across each short edge toward the center and leaving an opening for turning in the center. Turn the piece right side out and press it, pressing the opening seam allowances under. Topstitch close to all edges.

2. With wrong sides together, trim the back corners of the bottom panel to match the top panel. Fold each tie in half crosswise and baste the folded edge to the back edge of the bottom panel, 4" (10.2 cm) from the side edges.

3. Sew the top panel to the bottom panel with right sides together, leaving a 3" (7.6 cm) opening in the center of the back edge. Turn the panels right side out and press them.

4. Stuff the cushion with polyester fiberfill. Slip-stitch the opening closed.

5. Mark the center of the top panel and the center of the bottom panel. Follow the manufacturer's instructions to cover buttons with the fabric of your choice. Cut an 18" (45.7 cm) length of waxed button thread and slide one button shank onto the center of the thread. Insert both thread ends through the eye of the upholstery needle. Stitch through the cushion, inserting the needle at the center mark on the top panel and bringing it back out at the center mark on the bottom panel. Remove the needle. Slide the shank of the remaining button onto one thread end and tie the ends together. Pull the thread ends until the buttons indent the center of the cushion. Knot the thread ends securely under the bottom button; then trim them so they are hidden under the button.

7

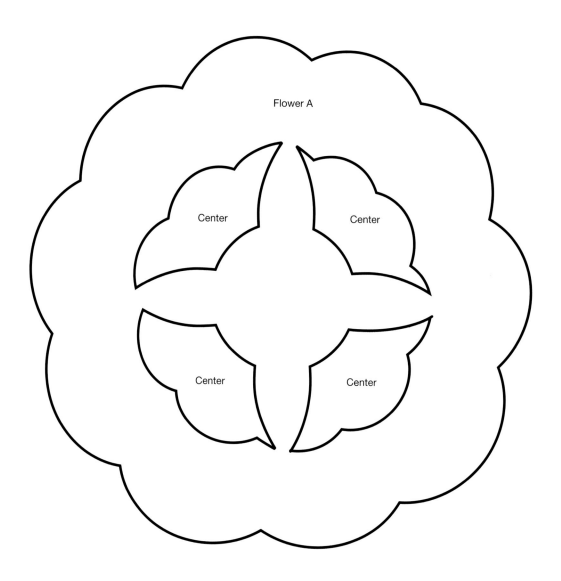

Flower A

Center

Center

Center

Center

Flower B

Flower C
Center

Raw–edge–appliqué Pillow

Combine fabric motifs with thread-painted flowers and leaves when you make this raw-edge-appliqué pillow. After fusing the motifs in place, you stitch the edges; then you fill in the details with free-motion stitching. If you want the edges to fray, cut the fusible-web shape slightly smaller than the motif before fusing it to the wrong side.

MATERIALS

Fabrics

⅝ yd (0.6 m) of 44" (111.8 cm)- or 54" (137.2 cm)-wide print decorator fabric for pillow front and back

½ yd (0.5 m) of fabric with motifs to cut out

¼ yd (0.2 m) of coordinating fabric for the welting

large scraps of coordinating solid fabrics for thread-painted flowers and leaves

Other Supplies

19" × 19" (48.3 × 48.3 cm) square of fusible tear-away stabilizer

four 9" × 12" (22.9 × 30.5 cm) sheets of double-stick fusible web

2¼ yd (2.1 m) of ³⁄₁₆" (5 mm) cotton cording or fusible piping

disappearing transfer paper

30-wt. cotton thread in coordinating colors

18" × 18" (45.7 × 45.7 cm) pillow form

Finished Size

18" × 18" (45.7 × 45.7 cm)

Cutting and Appliqués

1. From the decorator fabric, cut two 19" × 19" (48.3 × 48.3 cm) squares for the pillow front and back. From the contrasting fabric for the piping, cut 1⅜" (3.5 cm)-wide bias strips and piece them to 40" (101.5 c m) long.

2. Cut flower and leaf shapes from the solid fabrics. Cut out the fabric motifs of your choice. The pillow shown features three 4" × 5" (10.2 × 12.7 cm) floral motifs and eight leaves ranging from 3" to 5" (7.6 to 12.7 cm) long.

3. Following the instructions for fused reverse appliqué (page 53), trace and apply fusible web to the wrong side of each motif.

4. Fuse the stabilizer to the wrong side of the pillow front panel. Remove the paper backing from each appliqué motif and arrange them on the right side of the pillow front as shown in the photo. Fuse the motifs in place. Using disappearing transfer paper, transfer the detail lines of the thread-painted flowers and leaves onto the appliqués, if desired. You can also sketch them as you stitch instead of transferring the lines first.

5. Set your sewing machine for free-motion stitching (page 26). Stitch around the inside of each appliqué edge; then stitch the detail lines. For the stems between the appliqués, stitch back and forth until they are approximately ¼" (6 mm) wide. When you are finished stitching, tear away the excess stabilizer on the wrong side.

Assembly

1. To make the welting, refer to the instructions for making welting or piping (page 84). Wrap the bias strip right side out around the piping with the piping edges even. Fuse in place for fusible piping or use a zipper foot and baste close to the cord for regular piping.

2. Begin in the center of one edge on the right side of either pillow panel and pin the welting to the pillow panel with raw edges even. Using a zipper foot, begin 1" (2.5 cm) from the end of the welting and stitch it in place to ½" (1.3 cm) from the corner. Put the needle down in the fabric and lift the presser foot. Clip the piping seam allowance to the stitching line and pivot to turn the corner. Continue stitching to the next corner and repeat clipping the seam allowance and turning the corner.

3. To end the welting, stop stitching 2" (5 cm) from the beginning end. Pull back the fabric to reveal the cord and trim the cord even with the beginning end. Trim the extending fabric to 1½" (3.8 cm) past the beginning end. Turn the raw edge under ½" (1.3 cm) and wrap around the beginning end. Finish stitching the welting in place.

4. With right sides together and the panel with the piping on top, sew the front and back panels together, stitching on or just inside the welting stitching line. Leave 10" (25.4 cm) open in the center of the bottom edge. Turn the piece right side out and press, pressing the opening seam allowances under.

5. Insert the pillow form and slip-stitch the opening closed.

Dimensional-appliqués Throw

I love working with boiled wool felt; you can shape it and cut it without raveling, and its thick texture adds interest and dimension to all sorts of projects, including dimensional appliqués. For this project, they team up with whimsical trims to embellish a purchased cotton throw.

MATERIALS

Fabrics

purchased cotton throw, approximately 48" × 60" (121.9 × 152.4 cm)

½ yd (0.5 m) each of orange, dark red, lavender, purple, and green 36" (91.4 cm) -wide wool felt

Other Supplies

¾ yd (0.5 m) of ½" (1.3 cm)-wide, double-fold, green, pindot bias tape (or make your own)

½ yd (0.5 m) of ½" (1.3 cm)-wide, green, pindot rickrack

1½ yd (1.4 m) of 1¼" (3.2 cm) green maxi rickrack

six beads in assorted sizes for flower centers

waxed button thread

permanent fabric adhesive

washing machine and dryer

Boiling the Wool Felt

1. Separate the light and dark wool felt colors. Wash and dry like colors together.

2. Place the felt in a washing machine and wash on a regular cycle in warm water. Place it in a dryer and dry on high heat until almost dry. Remove from the dryer and lay it flat to dry completely.

Note: If you want wrinkles for some appliqués such as the leaves, leave the felt in the dryer until completely dry. If color remains in your washer or dryer, wash and dry an old terrycloth towel to remove it.

Making Flowers

1. Trace the patterns (page 69) onto paper and cut out.

2. Place the large flower pattern on the orange felt and trace around its edges with a fabric marker. Repeat to trace another large flower and six large flower centers. Cut out the pieces.

3. Use the medium flower pattern to cut two red flowers and one lavender flower. Use the medium flower center/ small flower pattern to cut two lavender flower centers, one red flower center, and one purple flower.

4. To make each large flower, layer two centers on top of a flower, alternating the petals on the center layers. Stitch the center of the layers together with ½" (1.3 cm)-long straight stitch.

5. Fold the flower in half with the center on the inside and mark the center point of the fold. Stitch a half circle around the center to shape the flower center. Use waxed button thread to hand sew a bead in the center of the flower, knotting the thread ends securely on the back. If you want the flower to have more dimension, use waxed button thread to stitch small tucks around the flower center on the back.

2

4

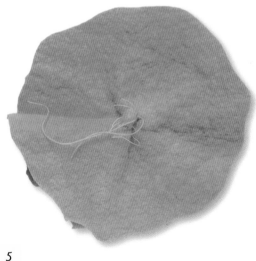

5

6. Fold each medium flower, medium-flower center, and the small flower in half. Beginning and ending ½"–1" (1.3–2.5 cm) from the outer edges, stitch ⅛" (3 mm) from the fold. Open the flower and fold it in half again with the stitched line running perpendicular to the fold.

7. Tack each medium flower center to a medium flower with several stitches through the center of both layers. Use waxed button thread to hand-sew a bead in the center of the flower, knotting the thread ends securely on the back.

8. Sew a bead to the center of the small purple flower, knotting the thread ends on the back.

7.

Assembly

1. Place the end of the throw to be embellished on a flat surface. Refer to the photo and arrange the flowers across the edge. Glue the centers of the flowers in place and let the adhesive dry. Cut a piece of bias tape or fabric rickrack for each stem and pin it in place. Stitch the bias tape stems in place with decorative stitches and the rickrack stems in place with straight stitches.

2. Freehand cut two green felt leaves for each flower, varying shapes and sizes as desired. Stitch a leaf on both sides of each stem, stitching from the base of the leaf and stopping approximately 1" (2.5 cm) from the tip.

8.

3. Cut a strip of rickrack 2" (5 cm) longer than the edge of the throw. Wrapping 1" (2.5 cm) on each end to the back of the throw, zigzag stitch the rickrack in place along the edge.

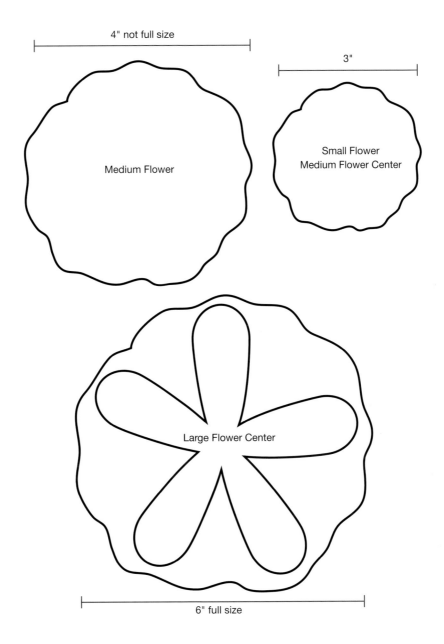

4" not full size

3"

Medium Flower

Small Flower
Medium Flower Center

Large Flower Center

6" full size

TRIM TIME

Trims provide one of the easiest ways to add embellishment to a project. You can add surface design and sometimes seam or edge finishes with decorative trims like fringes, gimp, braid, cording, bias tape or tubes, decorative threads, strings of small beads, yarn, and ribbon. And don't overlook the potential of using buttons, grommets, individual beads, and zippers as embellishments in addition to their practical applications.

Techniques

SURFACE EMBELLISHMENT WITH COUCHING

I love the freedom that couching allows when it comes to adding a surface design with cords and yarn. In general, if the trim is narrow and you can stitch it in place with a zigzag stitch or other decorative stitch with a zigzag motion, you can use it for couching. Better yet, if you have a cording, pearls and beads, braid, or couching foot for your machine that accommodates the trim, you can guide and stitch the trim in place as you sew.

Couching is an ideal way to accent the design lines of a fabric motif, to add your own design lines to a fabric motif or printed fabric background, or to create original design lines on solid-color fabric. To ensure success, keep the following tips in mind:

Fabric Selection

You can use most fabrics for couching when paired with trim in an appropriate weight. For best results, use only lighter-weight cord, yarn, or decorative thread on lightweight fabrics. Use a wider variety of trim weights on medium- and heavyweight fabric.

Fabric Preparation

The most important key to successfully adding any embellishment to a fabric surface is to make sure the fabric is stable and won't pucker or pull when you couch the trim in place. Heavier weights like faux suede and some decorator fabrics may be fine, but to ensure stability on most fabrics, apply fusible interfacing to the wrong side. Always test a scrap of fabric with the intended trim to determine if you need additional interfacing. You also can use stabilizers but use them with caution. Cut-away stabilizers may add unwanted thickness and zigzag stitches in the longer lengths used for couching can easily pull out when removing tear-away stabilizer. Cut the fabric to be embellished slightly larger than needed to allow for any take-up that may occur.

Trim Selection

Make sure the trim is compatible with the fabric weight and the machine foot you will be using. Wider cords, yarns, and braids are ideal for creating designs, while smaller ones are good for subtle

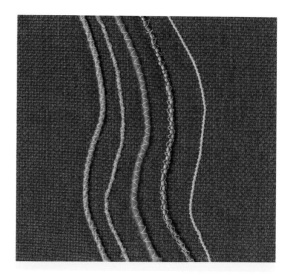

accents. For twisted cords and yarns, secure the ends with tape and twist as you sew to make sure they won't unravel.

Needle and Thread Selection

Use the needle size appropriate to the fabric and thread you will be using. Decide if you want the thread to stand out, blend with the trim, or be invisible and choose the thread accordingly.

Foot Selection

Use the machine presser foot appropriate to the trim you will be adding. For flat trims, a clear, open-toe, or zigzag foot is ideal. For rounded trims, use the specialty foot best suited to the trim size and shape.

Stitch Length and Width

Test the stitch you're planning to use with the trim to achieve the best results. For most trims, a medium-to-wide zigzag stitch is best. The thread

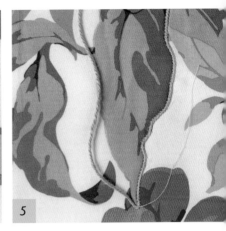
4

5

should be smooth and flat across the trim, without any puckering. It should completely cover the trim without excess stitch width but also not pierce the trim as you stitch.

Embellishing Fabric Design

1. Cut the piece of fabric slightly larger than needed. Stabilize the wrong side with fusible interfacing.

2. If desired, use a fabric marker or chalk pencil to outline the motifs or draw the design lines you want to couch.

3. Set up the machine with the appropriate needle, thread, and foot.

4. If you will stitch the trim ends into seams, begin at the edge of the fabric. If you won't, begin applying the trim in the least obvious area. Start at one end of the trim and sew slowly, allowing the foot to guide the trim and making sure it stays centered under the stitching.

5. To turn a corner, stop with the needle down in the fabric at the corner, lift the foot, and continue stitching.

6. To end the couching, cut the trim at the edge of the fabric if you will sew it into a seam. If you won't sew the ends into a seam, use a hand-sewing needle to stitch threads or lightweight yarn or cords to the wrong side of the fabric and knot it. Secure the knot with a dot of fabric adhesive.

6A. For heavier trims, overlap or abut the ends and stitch across the joined ends several times to secure them. If desired, reinforce the joined ends with a dab of fabric adhesive.

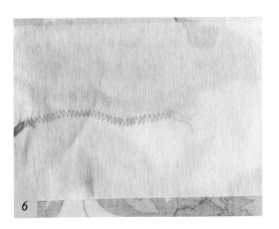
6

6a

Creating Couched Designs

Create free-form designs, add complementary design lines to fabric motifs, or attach raw-edge appliqués.

1. To create a free-form design, use a fabric marker or chalk pencil and draw the design lines on the surface of the fabric.

2. Follow Steps 3 through 6 for Embellishing Fabric Designs (above) to couch trim onto the marked lines.

To attach a dimensional appliqué to the surface with couched trim, pin the appliqué in place or secure it with a dab of fabric adhesive. Mark the line for the couched trim; then follow Steps 3 through 6 for embellishing fabric designs (page 73) to couch the trim onto the marked line.

SURFACE DESIGNS WITH TRIMS

Let trims do the talking when you use them to create the surface design for a fabric. You can use trims too wide or dimensional for couching and add them in a variety of ways.

Fringe and Tassel Trims

Fringes and tassel trims are available from basic to elaborate, and you can use them for elegant surface embellishment. Be sure to select styles of trim that have a decorative header—or lip—instead of ones intended to be sewn into a seam. If the trim doesn't have a decorative header, you can stitch it in place and then cover the header with a decorative flat trim.

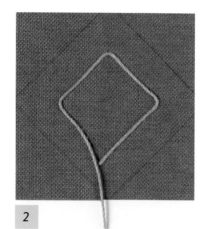

2

1

2

You can use ribbon or trim with a gathered edge for making flowers or rosettes. Make them directly on the fabric to be embellished or make them on a piece of felt and sew them onto the fabric as follows:

1. Plan the trim placement. Use a fabric marker or chalk pencil to draw lines onto the fabric or plan to use the trim to accent edges or piecing seams. You can also achieve a decorator look by stitching parallel lines of a pretty trim across a pillow panel or across the ends of a table runner.

2. Instead of using pins, apply self-adhesive, double-sided basting tape, or fusible web tape to the center of the wrong side of the trim header. These tapes ensure that the trim stays straight during stitching, as the edges may shift between pins.

3. Stitch the trim in place along both long edges of the header.

Flat and Low-dimension Trims

You can use flat trims—such as braid, gimp, ribbon, or bias tape—or decorative trims with a slight amount of dimension for the same types of designs as fringe or tassel trims, and they are more versatile when it comes to creating curved shapes. You can stitch them flat in place, along one or both edges. You can also gather one or both edges on trim that is lightweight or medium-weight to create dimensional effects and designs.

Attaching Flat Trims

1. Plan the trim placement. Use a fabric marker or chalk pencil to draw lines onto the fabric or plan to use the trim to accent the edge of a fabric motif or appliqué or to cover or accent seams. Depending on the trim's width, you can use it for curved as well as straight designs; the narrower the trim, the more intricate the details you can create with it.

2. Instead of using pins, apply self-adhesive, double-sided basting tape, or fusible-web tape to the center of the trim's wrong side. These tapes ensure that the trim stays straight during stitching, as the edges may shift between pins.

3. Stitch the trim in place along one or both long edges.

Dimensional Designs

Ribbon and light- to medium-weight, woven trims are best-suited for dimensional designs because they are easy to gather. Avoid heavier trims that will be too bulky when gathered.

1. For ribbon with a wired edge, slide the ribbon back from the end of the wire at one end. Bend the wire end over the edge of the ribbon several times to secure it. Slide the ribbon along the wire, pushing it toward the secured end and gathering the edge to the length desired. Secure the remaining end in the same manner as the beginning end.

2. For ribbon without a wired edge and other trims, sew a gathering stitch close to one edge. Pull the bobbin thread to gather the edge to the desired length, then knot the thread ends together at each end to secure the thread. You can also gather the center of the ribbon in this manner.

3. Stitch the gathered edge or center of the ribbon to the fabric surface as desired, creating straight or curved lines, covering seams, or accenting fabric motifs. Sew slowly, using the tip of your scissors to evenly guide the gathers under the presser foot as needed.

Gather the trim close to one long edge. Fold the short ends securely under the bottom edge of the fold, with the trim wire or with stitching.

Hand-stitch one end of the ribbon to the fabric for the center. Wrap the gathered edge into a spiral around the center, hand-stitching the gathered edge in place as you wrap. Finish the center with a button if desired.

FABRIC TUBES

Use fabric tubes to make a variety of surface designs. Press them flat and use them in the same manner as other flat trims, fill them with cording to couch in place, shape them into loops, or use them for ties or laces. Fabric tubes are easy to make in a variety of sizes, especially when you use a tube-turning tool. For smaller tube sizes or tubes that you will use for making curved designs, cut the fabric for the tube on the bias instead of the straight or cross grain.

Basic Fabric Tubes

1. To make a basic fabric tube, cut the fabric in the desired length, piecing strips together if needed to achieve the length. The width should be double the finished width of the tube, plus ½" (1.3 cm) for seam allowances. Cut the fabric on the bias for smaller tube sizes or those that you will use for creating curved designs. You can cut fabric strips for larger tubes on the bias or straight grain.

2. With right sides together, sew the long edges together using a ¼" (6 mm) seam allowance. Instead of a straight stitch, use a short, very slight zigzag stitch to help prevent the seam from ripping during the turning process. Trim the seam allowance to ⅛" (3 mm) on narrow tubes.

3. If the tube is wide enough, turn it right side out by hand, or if it is narrow, pin a safety pin to one end and work it through the tube, pulling it right side out. For easy turning, use a tube-turning tool and follow the manufacturer's instructions.

Filled Fabric Tubes

Two easy ways exist to cover cording with a fabric tube for use as a decorative surface embellishment. You can couch smaller filled tubes onto your project by machine or attach larger tubes by hand.

For the first technique:

1. To cover cording by machine, begin with a length of cotton filler cord that is twice as long as the finished length you need. Cut the fabric strip in the length and width needed to cover the cord, adding ½" (1.3 cm) to the cord diameter for the seam allowances. Wrap the fabric around one end of the cord with the wrong side out and raw edges even. Use a zipper foot and stitch the fabric edges together ⅛" (3 mm) from the cord. Sew across the inside end of the tube.

2. Begin at the stitched end and slide the fabric over the cording, turning the tube right side out. Cut away the excess cording.

For the second technique:

1. To cover cording using a tube turning tool, follow the Basic Fabric Tube instructions to make a fabric tube. With the tube wrong side out, insert the cylinder and use the hook to pull about ½" (1.3 cm) of the fabric into the cylinder.

2. Hold the end of the cording at the cylinder end and continue pulling the fabric through the tube; the fabric will grab the cording and pull it through; do not grab the cording with the hook.

MAKING BIAS TAPE OR TUBE DESIGNS ON STABILIZER

Because tubes or flat trims made with bias strips are easy to shape, they are ideal for creating into freestanding designs on a background of fabric-like, water-soluble stabilizer. After stitching the background, you wash the stabilizer away, leaving only the trim design. Use these designs as freestanding accents for necklines, cuffs, and other edges or for surface accents.

1. For a straight edge, draw two lines equal to the width and length of the finished border onto the paper backing of the fabric-like, water-soluble stabilizer. For a shaped edge, draw the shape's length and desired border width onto the stabilizer. Cut out the border area along the marked lines.

2. To be secure when you finish the piece, all trim pieces must overlap, and the outside edges must also be trimmed. Do not leave any loose end, corners, or curves. Arrange the trim design on the stabilizer strip. Finish the edges with bias tape wrapped around the edge or on top.

3. Begin with the outside strip and stitch along both edges of all trim pieces.

4. Remove the stabilizer with water, following the manufacturer's instructions. Only the trim design will remain.

5. Topstitch one edge of the trim onto the edge of the garment.

SURFACE DESIGN WITH NOTIONS

Now that you've discovered how much fun it is to add surface designs with trims, consider adding notions like grommets, buttons, or zippers to your embellishment repertoire. Used alone or with other trims or fabric manipulation techniques, these details often add the perfect finishing touch.

Buttons

Buttons are so much fun to use and can be wildly creative. In addition to the wonderful array of buttons you can find at your local fabric or quilt shops, many artists make ceramic, porcelain, dichroic glass, and other artful buttons and sell them online. Vintage buttons, too, are interesting to collect and use, and you can find them at antique shows as well as sewing expos and online. You can also style your own buttons when you purchase covered-button forms to cover with fabric or layer buttons in assorted colors and styles.

Here are a few tips for designing with buttons:

• Embellish clothing and accessories. Highlight a sweater neckline with an assortment of single-color or mixed buttons. Apply fusible tricot interfacing to the wrong side of the area to be embellished. Arrange the buttons and mark their placement or the design outline with a fabric marker or chalk pencil; then sew the buttons in place by machine or hand. Also consider adding button designs to jacket collars or pockets, blouse collars, skirt hems, the front of a dress, or tote bags.

• Create free-form designs or accent fabric motifs on pillows, valances, wall quilts, and other home-décor accessories. Apply fusible interfacing to the wrong side of the fabric. Arrange the buttons in a design on the right side of the fabric.

• Use a fine-tip fabric marker to mark the button placements on the fabric through the holes of the buttons. Remove the buttons. Sew them in place, aligning the buttons with the marks.

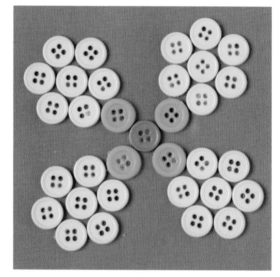

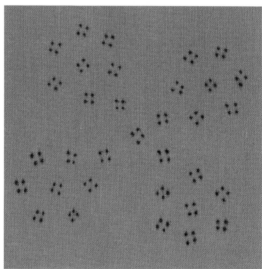

- Layer buttons in assorted colors and sizes by aligning the holes and hand stitching them in place.

- Or layer them with felt or faux-suede circles, squares, or other shapes.

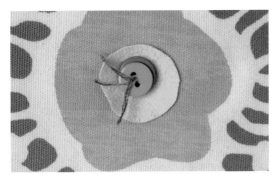

- Accent designs. Use a decorative button to finish the center of a yo-yo, appliqué, or dimensional flower made from ribbon.

Button Tufting

Tufting with buttons is a practical and attractive finishing touch for pillows, cushions, quilts, soft headboards, and ottomans. You will need two buttons with shanks or large holes and waxed button thread for each tuft. You will also need an upholstery needle that is long enough to stitch through the project. To add tufting:

1. Mark corresponding placement marks on the top and bottom of the project to be tufted. Cut a long length of waxed button thread. Center the shank of one button on the thread or slide the button holes onto the center of the thread. Insert both ends of the thread through the eye of an upholstery needle that is long enough to stitch through the project.

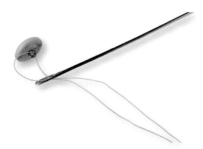

1

2. Stitch through the top of the project at the mark, bringing the needle out at the corresponding mark on the bottom.

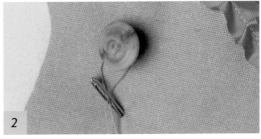

2

3. Remove the needle and insert one thread through the remaining button shank or both ends of the thread through the button holes. Tie the thread ends together, pulling tightly to indent the surface. Knot the thread securely. Trim the thread ends at least ¼" (6 mm) from the knot.

3

Grommets and Eyelets

Like buttons, grommets and eyelets offer a myriad of design possibilities in addition to their practical applications. Both are available in a variety of sizes and styles, and setting applications also vary. Eyelets usually consist of one piece that separates at the bottom when you apply it, while grommets are usually two pieces that interlock when set. Recommended setting techniques range from pliers and setting tools to simply snapping the sections together. Always follow the manufacturer's recommendations for marking and setting the eyelets or grommets that you plan to use.

Let your imagination soar and use grommets or eyelets to accent garments and accessory edges, make free-form designs, and accent fabric motifs or machine-embroidered designs. You can also line the inside of large grommets with contrasting fabric or use them to attach dimensional appliqués. Consider the following tips and ideas when planning your embellishments:

• Use fabric that is tightly woven or knit. Apply interfacing to the wrong side to prevent the grommets or eyelets from pulling out. Nonwoven fabrics like faux suede, faux leather, and wool felt are also ideal. You can also apply ribbon or twill tape to either side of the fabric as reinforcement.

• Arrange the grommets or eyelets on the fabric to determine the spacing and design. Mark the center of each hole with a fabric marker.

• Large grommets are available in decorative colors and shapes for projects that can enhance your home. Use them to add a practical and decorative touch to the top edges of curtains, valances, shower curtains, and other fabric panels that you will hang on a rod.

• Replace a traditional buttoned or zipped closure, or accent seams with grommets and laced ribbon or cording.

• Create a design on the edges of garments, accessories, table linens, curtain panels, and more with grommets. Add lacing around the edge and through the holes if desired.

• Apply assorted sizes or colors to the fabric surface to create a free-form design.

• Accent fabric motifs or machine-embroidered designs with grommets or eyelets.

• Cut out contrasting fabric and glue it to the back of larger grommets with the right side showing through the opening.

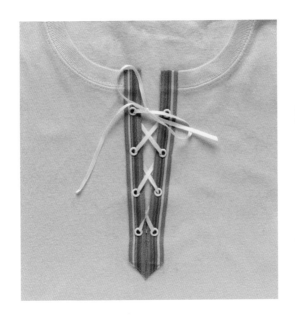

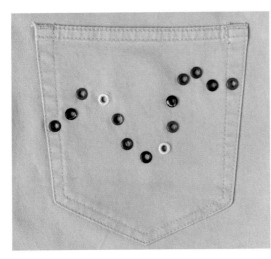

Zippers

Like buttons and grommets, manufacturers originally designed zippers with a practical purpose in mind, but they offer a lot of creative potential. Manufacturers are even jumping on the fashion trend of exposed zippers and making zippers with fun novelty tapes and specialty teeth or pulls. Try some of the following ideas to turn practical into pretty:

• Use a long separating zipper with brass or aluminum teeth to accent the edge of a collar or front edges of a jacket, or to insert in the seam of a pieced pillow. Separate the zipper and use a zipper foot to stitch the tape to the wrong side or the inside of a seam with the teeth extending along the edge.

• Replace any traditional zipper closure or add a surface embellishment with an exposed zipper that has decorative tape. Simply finish the closure edges and apply the zipper to the right side.

• Accent the edge of ribbon, bias tape, or an appliqué by sewing a separating zipper tape to the wrong side with the teeth along the edge.

Dimensional Accents

Use zippers to make dimensional accents. Using the sides of a separating zipper individually, create loops, twisted edges, flowers, or other shapes.

To make flower petals using a separating zipper with decorative tapes, begin with 24" (61 cm)-long zipper and a 1" (2.5 cm)-diameter circle of felt.

1. Cut one tape into five 4" (10.2 cm) lengths. Sew a gathering stitch along the edge of each tape, shape a petal, and pull the gathering threads to gather the edge.

2. Tack the bottom of a petal to the felt circle.

3. Overlap and sew the bottom edges of the remaining petals to the felt. Sew a button to the center.

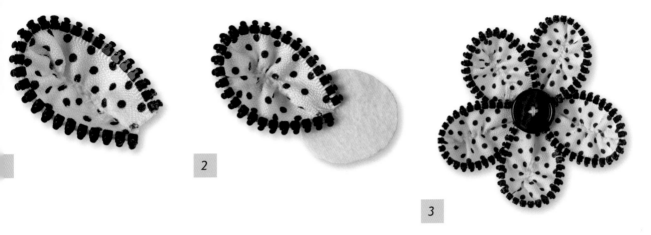

To make a rose, begin with a 3" × 3" (7.6 × 7.6 cm) square of felt and a zipper of any length that has a decorative tape; the finished size will depend on the length of the zipper. One zipper will make two roses.

1. Stitch a gathering stitch along one edge of the zipper tape. Pull the threads to gather the edge and knot the thread ends to secure them.

2. Begin at one end and roll the tape in a spiral, whipstitching or gluing the tape edges to the felt to form the rose.

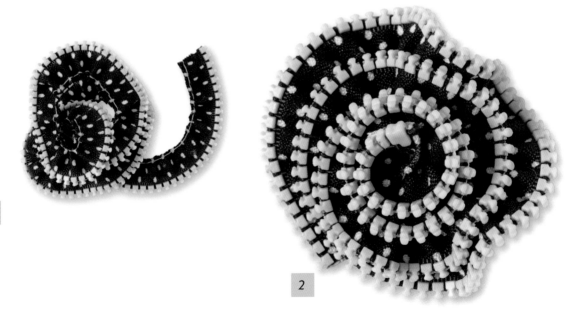

EDGE AND SEAM EMBELLISHMENTS

Dress up seams and edges when you finish them with piping, purchased trim, or other embellishments.

Purchased trims abound for finishing edges. You can add a beautiful finish to the edge of pillows, window treatments, table linens, bed linens, and chair or ottoman skirts with a gorgeous tasseled trim or a fringe with a decorative header. Rickrack can add a touch of whimsy to throws, placemats, or curtains. You can also layer more than one trim and sew them onto the edge as one, to create a unique look.

To add purchased trim to a finished edge, pin the header in place or adhere it to the edge with basting tape or fusible-web tape. Stitch in place along both long edges of a wide header or use a wide zigzag stitch to sew narrow trims in place. For trim like rickrack or other novelty shapes, stitch it in place along the center of the trim using a narrow zigzag stitch or straight stitch.

Give a basic seam a designer look when you add twisted cord with a lip, welting, or other seam embellishments such as ribbon or bias tape inserted in the seam.

Making Welting or Piping

Welting and piping are terms often used interchangeably. They are essentially the same—fabric-covered cotton cord with a fabric edge for inserting in a seam—and add a professional-looking finish to many home-décor projects and garments. It is often called piping when used on garments or fashion accessories and welting when used for home-décor applications. In general, you will use smaller cording for fashion applications and larger sizes for home-décor projects. For any size of cording, cover it as follows:

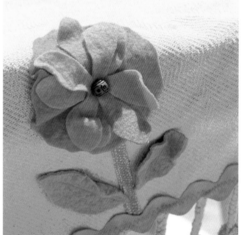

1. Determine the cut width of the fabric strip by measuring around the cord and adding 1" (2.5 cm) for seam allowances. The length of the fabric strip should be the finished length of the corded edge plus 3" (7.6 cm) for overlapping. Cut a bias strip of fabric in the determined dimensions.

2. Wrap the fabric strip around the cording with the right side out and edges even. Use a zipper foot and baste the edges together ⅜" (1 cm) from the edge.

3. To add the welting to a seam, pin or use basting tape to adhere it to the right side of one fabric panel with the edges even. Begin sewing 1" (2.5 cm) from the end of the welting and stitch it in along the welting basting line. For a pillow or other panel with corners, stitch the welting in place to ½" (1.3 cm) from the corner. Put the needle down in the fabric and lift the presser foot. Clip the welting seam allowance to the stitching line and pivot to turn the corner.

Continue stitching to the next corner and repeat clipping the seam allowance and turning the corner.

4. To end the welting, stop stitching 2" (5 cm) from the beginning end. Pull back the fabric to reveal the cord and trim the cord even with the beginning end. Trim the extending fabric to 1½" (3.8 cm) past the beginning end. Turn the raw edge under ½" (1.3 cm) and wrap around the beginning end. Finish stitching the welting in place.

5. With right sides together and the panel with the welting on top, stitch the fabric panels together using a regular stitch length and a ½" (1.3 cm) seam allowance. Leave an opening for turning if applicable to the project.

Twisted Cording with Lip

Twisted cording adds a similar look and is applied in the same manner as welting. To add it to a seam, be sure to sew it to a lip (fabric strip).

1. Pin or use basting tape to adhere the cording lip to the right side of one fabric panel with the edges even. Using a zipper foot, begin stitching 1" (2.5 cm) from the end of the cording to baste the lip to the fabric ³⁄₈" (1 cm) from the edge. For a pillow or other panel with corners, stitch it in place to ½" (1.3 cm) from the corner. Put the needle down in the fabric and lift the presser foot. Clip the lip to the stitching line and pivot to turn the corner. Continue stitching to the next corner and repeat clipping the seam allowance and turning the corner.

2. To finish the ends with smaller cords, overlap the ends and sew them into the seam or join them for a continuous look. Larger cords are often too heavy to be overlapped and should be joined as follows:

1. To join the cording ends, cut the cording end 2" (5 cm) longer than the beginning end. Clip the stitching, holding it onto the lip, and wrap tape around the individual cord ends to prevent raveling. Repeat for the beginning end.

2. Overlap the sets of ends to appear continuous.

3. Wrap the top lip over the cord ends and finish sewing to the edge.

4. With right sides together and the panel with the cording on top, stitch the fabric panels together using a regular stitch length and a ½" (1.3 cm) seam allowance. Leave an opening for turning if applicable to the project.

Embellished Jacket

Embellish a jacket, sweater, shirt, or other garment with trim arranged in the design of your choice. Sticky water-soluble stabilizer makes it easy to arrange the trim design as you please; then it provides stability as you stitch it on the garment. It is especially useful for knits that might distort if you stitched the trims directly onto the fabric. The jacket shown displays a new sense of style with its updated, zipper-trimmed collar.

MATERIALS

jacket or other garment of your choice

Other Supplies

tracing cloth or clear, water-soluble stabilizer

transfer paper

sticky, fabric-like, water-soluble stabilizer

double-fold bias tape or other narrow trim

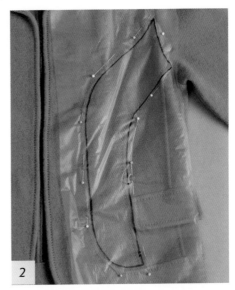

Instructions

1. Select an area of the garment to embellish. Collars, pockets, plackets, cuffs, and necklines are ideal for accenting, as are pieced areas formed by princess seams and yokes.

2. Pin tracing cloth or clear, water-soluble stabilizer over the area to be embellished. Trace the outline of the area.

3. Use transfer paper and transfer the traced lines onto the paper side of the fabric-like, sticky stabilizer. Cut the shape out.

4. Remove the paper backing from the stabilizer. Refer to the instructions for making trim designs (page 77) and arrange the bias tape or other trim on the sticky surface. Press the trim firmly in place.

5. Pin the stabilizer with the design onto the garment. Stitch along both edges of the trim, forming the design outline. Stitch both edges of all remaining pieces of trim.

6. Remove the stabilizer with water, following the manufacturer's instructions.

Embellished Motifs Pillow

This ikat fabric with alternating 12" (30.5 cm)-long motifs is perfect for showcasing a variety of trims. The long, continuous lines provide good guidelines for couching the burlap cording and the small circular motifs are just the right size for button embellishments. On the back, flat trim embellished with buttons creates the illusion of a closure, and a purchased burlap appliqué and trim with a lip add the finishing touches.

MATERIALS

Fabrics

⅝ yd (0.6 m) of 54" (137.2 cm)-wide decorator fabric with large-scale motifs

Other Supplies

½ yd (0.5 m) of fusible interfacing

jute cord in sufficient ydage for outlines to be couched

buttons in size and number to correspond with fabric motifs and embellish back trim

⅝ yd (0.6 m) of ½" (1.3 cm)-wide, flat, jute trim

3" (7.6 cm)-diameter natural jute appliqué

2⅛ yd (1.9 m) of trim with lip for edges

18" × 18" (45.7 × 45.7 cm) pillow form

couching foot or pearls and beads foot

Finished Size

18" × 18" (45.7 × 45.7 cm)

Cutting and Trim Application

1. From the fabric, cut one 20" × 20" (50.8 × 50.8 cm) square for the front, with a centered motif, and one 19" × 19" (48.3 × 48.3 cm) square for the back. Cut one 20" × 20" (50.8 × 50.8 cm) square from the fusible interfacing and fuse it to the wrong side of the front fabric square.

2. To embellish the front panel, follow the instructions for embellishing fabric designs (page 73) to couch the trim along the motif lines of your choice, using the foot to guide the trim as you sew.

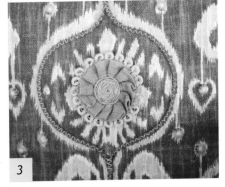

3

3. Sew the appliqué to the center motif. Sew buttons onto the smaller motifs. Trim the panel to 19" × 19" (48.3 × 48.3 cm).

4. To embellish the back panel, sew the flat trim to the center of the panel along both long edges. Sew evenly-spaced buttons onto the trim.

4

5. Follow the instructions for adding trim to a seam (page 74) and sew the trim to the front panel. Sew the panels together with right sides facing and a ½" (1.3 cm) seam allowance, leaving an opening for turning. Insert the pillow form and slip-stitch the opening closed.

Pillow with Trim Design

This decorator burlap fabric provides a good background for adding a trim design. The color is solid, allowing the design to show up, but it also has a nice texture that adds to the finished look of the pillow.

MATERIALS

Fabrics

½ yd (0.5 m) of 54" (137.2 cm)-wide decorator burlap fabric

Other Supplies

½ yd (0.5 m) of fusible interfacing

3 yd (2.7 m) of ⅞" (2.2 cm)-wide natural sisal flat trim

2 yd (1.8 m) of 2" (5 cm)-wide sisal fringe

buttons in size and number desired to accent couched design

3" (7.6 cm)-diameter natural jute appliqué

½" (1.3 cm)-wide double-stick fusible web tape

14" × 18" (35.6 × 45.7 cm) pillow form

Finished Size

14" × 18" (35.6 × 45.7 cm)

Cutting and Trim Application

1. From the fabric, cut two 15" × 19" (38.1 × 48.3 cm) rectangles for the front and back. Cut one 15" × 19" (38.1 × 48.3 cm) rectangle from the interfacing. Fuse the interfacing to the wrong side of one fabric panel for the front.

2. On the right side of the front panel, mark the center of each edge. Use a fabric marker and draw lines connecting the marks to form a diamond shape.

3. Apply fusible-web tape to the wrong side of the trim. Remove the paper backing and align trim along the marked lines on the front panel, folding at the corners. Cut the end ¾"(1.9 cm) past the beginning tape and wrap the end under the beginning end. Fuse the trim in place. Stitch along both long edges.

4. Apply a second row of trim 1½" (3.8 cm) inside the first row and fuse in place. Sew along both long edges.

5. Sew the appliqué to the center of the front panel and sew on buttons as desired.

6. Begin in the center of the front panel bottom edge and baste the trim around the edge, aligning the trim header to the fabric edge. Sew the panels together with right sides facing and a ½" (1.3 cm) seam allowance, leaving an opening for turning. Insert the pillow form and slip-stitch the opening closed.

2

FABRIC MANIPULATION

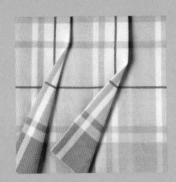 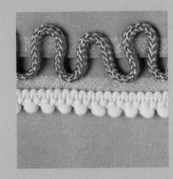 

What can make an already fabulous fabric even better? Fabric manipulation!
You can highlight a motif with trapunto or quilting, make fun yo-yos or
inserts with gathers, or transform a striped pattern with pleats. And that's just
the beginning. You can manipulate tucks into all kinds of interesting
designs, and you can texturize beautiful silk fabrics with crinkled pleats
or add a tactile touch with stuffed tufts or cut-felt loops.

Techniques

TRAPUNTO

This technique results in a raised area with a stitched outline and is ideal for adding dimension to a fabric motif or appliqué, creating a raised motif on solid-color fabric, or adding dimensional corded effects.

When selecting a fabric print, look for larger motifs with well-defined outlines. Small details tend to pucker when stuffed or not show up. A motif surrounded by a solid color will show up better than one placed on a background of other motifs.

Like any quilting technique, trapunto will make the finished size of the surface smaller. For best results, complete stitching and stuffing before cutting out the pieces for your project. Or cut them several inches larger to allow for the shrinking. If you will launder the finished project, prewash and dry the fabric before stitching.

1

Stuffed Designs

This technique is the original trapunto for quilting, and quilters usually combined it with hand stitching. You can achieve the same effects with machine-stitched edges and polyester fiberfill.

1. Select the fabric motif or appliqué you want to highlight or use a fabric pencil or marker to draw a motif on solid-color fabric. The motif should have clearly defined edges that will be easy to stuff.

2. If highlighting a single motif, cut a piece of muslin that is at least 1" (2.5 cm) larger all around than the motif. If you will be stitching many motifs, cut a piece of muslin that is the same size as the outer fabric. Baste the muslin to the wrong side of the fabric beneath the motif.

3. On the right side of the fabric, stitch along the outline of the motif.

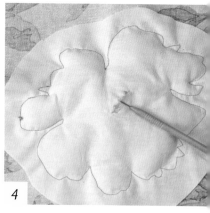

4

4. Turn the fabric over with the muslin side up. Cut a small slit in the center of the motif, being careful not to cut the top fabric. Use a stuffing tool to insert small pieces of fiberfill evenly into the opening. Do not overstuff, or the motif will pucker. Whipstitch the opening closed.

Padded Designs

This technique results in a similar look to stuffed designs. You layer high-loft batting and muslin on the wrong side of the motif to be highlighted.

1. Select the fabric motif or appliqué you want to highlight or use a fabric pencil or marker to draw the motif of your choice on solid-color fabric.

2. Cut a piece each of muslin and batting that is larger than the motif. Place the muslin on the bottom, layer the batting next, and place the fabric with the motif on top. Pin or baste the layers together.

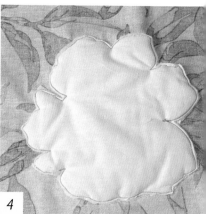

4

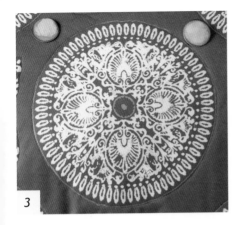

3

1

2

3. On the right side of the top fabric, stitch along the outline of the motif.

4. Turn the fabric over with the muslin side up. Carefully trim the muslin and batting away from the motif, cutting close to the stitching.

Faux Trapunto

For this technique, the motifs aren't actually stuffed individually. Rather, the entire fabric surface is backed with batting and muslin before motif outlines are stitched. The result is a more subtle dimensional effect with the entire surface padded. You can also stitch some of the larger detail lines of the motifs if desired.

1. Select the fabric motif or appliqué you want to highlight or use a fabric pencil or marker to draw the motif of your choice on solid-color fabric. The motif should have clearly-defined edges that will be easily highlighted with stitching.

2. Cut batting and muslin the same size as the top fabric. Pin or baste the layers together.

3. On the right side of the fabric, stitch along the outline of the motif. Do not cut away the batting or muslin.

Corded Designs

This type of trapunto adds dimension when you fill one or more stitched channels with cording or yarn. It shows up best on solid-color fabric and is a nice accent for edges or when combined with a trapunto, cutwork, or appliqué motif.

1. Determine the width of the columns to stitch based on the dimension of your yarn or cording; you can also use multiple strands. Use a fabric pencil or marker to draw the column of stitching lines on the right side of the fabric.

2. Cut a piece of muslin that is larger than the area with the columns. For a lightweight fabric where the muslin's edge may show, cut the muslin the same size as the top piece. Pin or baste it to the wrong side of the fabric. Stitch the layers together on the marked lines.

3. Thread a tapestry, upholstery, or other needle with a dull point and large eye with the yarn or cording. Working on the muslin side, use the needle to guide the yarn or cording through the channel. If the yarn or cord is fine enough, you can stitch into the channel; otherwise cut a small slit. Trim the ends slightly longer than the channel and apply a dab of seam sealant or permanent fabric adhesive to the ends to prevent fraying. Lightly glue the ends in place. For corners or angles, fill the adjoining channels separately.

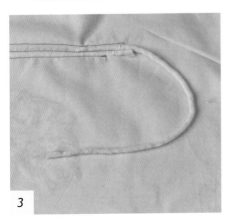

3

GATHERS

Gathers take on all sorts of shapes and sizes and you can use them to create fullness or ruffles for a wide range of sewing projects. But think beyond their basic applications to use gathers for creative applications like yo-yos or inserts.

Yo-Yos

Always a favorite with quilters, today yo-yos are sporting new looks and popping up on garments as well as fashion and home-décor accessories. Not only are they fun to make, but also you can combine them with other trims, showcase a contrasting fabric on the inside, layer assorted sizes, or stitch them onto other fabrics as individual accents or in rows for an overall effect.

It's easy to cut circles and make your own yo-yos by hand or machine in any size, but also templates are available for speeding the process and making novelty shapes like flowers, hearts, ovals, and butterflies. You can also make yo-yos by gathering the edges of ribbon or folded strips of fabric.

For any type of yo-yo, use all-purpose thread in the needle and heavy thread in the bobbin. Set your machine for a 10 mm–20 mm basting stitch or the longest straight stitch available. A longer stitch length will result in deeper gathers and a more tightly closed opening. A shorter stitch length will yield shallow gathers and a large opening.

Basic Yo-Yo

1. Decide the finished size of the yo yo. Cut a circle of fabric with a diameter that is twice the finished size, plus ½" (1.3 cm).

2. Press the circle's edge ¼" (6 mm) to the wrong side.

3. Sew a basting stitch around the edge, leaving the thread ends long.

4. Knot the ends of the needle threads together. Pull the ends of the bobbin threads to gather the edge and knot the threads securely together at the edge of the fabric. Arrange the gathers evenly with the opening in the center and press the yo-yo flat.

3

Yo-Yo with Contrasting Center

1. Decide the finished sizes of the yo-yo and its center opening. Subtract an amount ½" (1.3 cm) less than the diameter of the center opening from the finished size of the yo-yo, and cut a circle of fabric this size. Cut a circle of the contrasting fabric that is 1" (2.5 cm) larger than the opening.

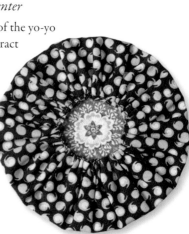

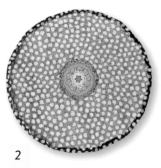

2

2. Fuse or sew the small fabric circle to the center of the wrong side of the large fabric circle. Press the large circle's edge ¼" (6 mm) to the wrong side.

3. Sew a 7 mm–10 mm basting stitch close to the edge, leaving the thread ends long. Knot the needle threads together. Pull the ends of the bobbin thread to gather the edge. Knot the bobbin threads securely. Trim the thread ends to 1" (2.5 cm) long and glue them to the inside of the opening.

4. Press the yo-yo flat with the opening centered. Whipstitch or glue the opening edges in place.

Fabric-strip Yo-Yo

These yo-yos look the same on both sides and are ideal for reversible projects where you want the gathers on both sides. For lightweight fabrics like silk taffeta, you can press under the edges that will be gathered for a finished opening. For cotton fabrics, either finish the raw edges with serging or plan to leave them raw and cover the opening with a button or a smaller circle with finished edges.

1. Decide the finished yo-yo size. You will fold the fabric strip in half and gather it, so you will need a fabric strip in a width that is equal to the radius of the yo-yo. You can also piece the fabric strip crosswise or lengthwise to add interest to the finished yo-yo. See the instructions for the yo-yo door hanger (page 114).

2. To determine the length of the fabric strip, decide on the amount of gathering you want. For medium gathers, plan to cut the strip approximately three times the yo-yo diameter as shown on the 7" (17.8 cm)-diameter yo-yo made with a 6" × 21" (15.2 × 53.3 cm) strip of fabric.

2A. For more gathers, cut the strip longer as shown on the 4" (10.2 cm)-diameter yo-yo made with a 3½" × 21" (8.9 × 53.3 cm) strip of fabric.

3. Cut a strip of fabric in the width and length determined in Steps 1 and 2.

4. Use a ¼" (6 mm) seam allowance to sew the short edges of the strip together with right sides facing. Press the seam open. Press the strip in half lengthwise with wrong sides facing.

2

5. Sew the raw edges together with a gathering stitch leaving the thread ends long. Knot the ends of the needle threads together. Pull the ends of the bobbin threads to gather the edge and knot the ends securely together.

6. Cover the raw opening edges with a button or a hemmed circle of fabric on each side.

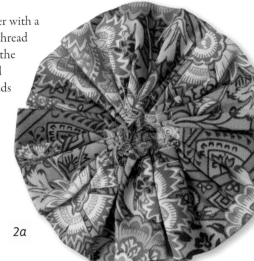

2a

Gathered Inserts

Add texture and an element of surprise to the surface of a project when you add gathered inserts of matching or contrasting fabric. Depending on the look you want, you can use a shaped insert to highlight a fabric motif or as a decorative element in a single panel of fabric.

To make a straight, gathered insert:

1. Cut a strip of fabric that is equal to the finished insert's width plus 1" (2.5 cm) and twice as long.

2. Sew a row of basting stitches ½" (1.3 cm) from each long edge of the fabric. Sew another row of basting stitches ⅜" (1 cm) from each long edge. Knot the thread's ends together on each side at one end.

3. Pull the ends of the bobbin threads to gather each edge to half of its original length. Knot the thread ends together at the end to secure the gathers.

4. With right sides together, use a ½" (1.3 cm) seam allowance to sew a fabric panel to each side of the gathered insert.

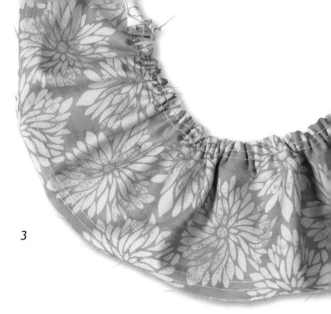

3

4

1

4

To make a gathered, shaped insert:

1. To make an insert without seams, mark the insert opening on the fabric. Cut the opening out ¼" (6 mm) inside the marked lines. Press the fabric under along the lines, clipping corners as needed.

2. Cut out an insert shape that is ½" (1.3 cm) longer and two to three times as wide as the opening. Sew a gathering stitch ¼" (6 mm) on the insert's long edges. Pull the basting thread ends to gather the edges to ½" (1.3 cm) wider than the opening; then knot the thread ends.

3. From the wrong side, center the insert in the opening. Secure the edges with self-adhesive basting tape.

4. On the right side, topstitch close to the opening edges.

PLEATS AND TUCKS

Oh, the fun you can have when you use pleats and tucks to highlight fabric patterns or to add texture and dimension to solid-color or subtly printed fabrics! So what is the difference between these two fabric-folding techniques? You fold pleats—box, inverted, or knife—and then stitch across one or both ends to secure the folds. On the other hand, you fold tucks and then stitch along the entire length of the fold.

Both pleats and tucks maintain their shape best and are easier to press if you spray the fabric lightly with starch before making the folds.

Box Pleats

Box pleats feature an inward fold on each side of the pleat. Each fold is usually half the width of the pleat with the folded edges meeting in the center back of the pleat. They are ideal for many home décor projects, including table skirts, ottomans, and window treatments. You can also add interest to garments and accessories or make ruffles with narrow versions of these pleats.

1. To determine the cut width of the fabric panel to be pleated, decide how many pleats you want and the total pleat allowance (pleat width + width of two folds). You can space the pleats closely or several inches apart, depending on the look you want. Add the pleat allowances and spaces between the pleats to determine the cut width, allowing extra fabric for seams or hems.

2. Mark the pleats and folds across the edge of the fabric. For pressed pleats, mark the fold line for the length of the pleat.

3. Fold and press the pleats at the marks, pressing the top edges only for soft pleats or the entire length for pressed pleats.

4. Baste across the top edge of the fabric to secure the pleats for a skirt or edge. For an insert or panel, stitch across the top and bottom edges.

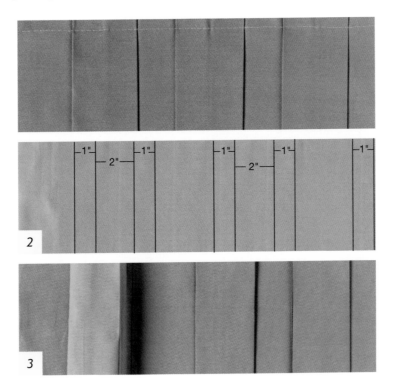

Inverted Pleats

Inverted pleats feature a fold on each side that meets in the center front of the pleat. Each side pleat is half the width of the inverted pleat. You plan and mark them the same way as box pleats but fold them in the opposite direction.

1. To determine the cut width of the fabric panel to be pleated, decide how many pleats you want and the total pleat allowance (pleat width + width of two folds). You can space the pleats closely or several inches apart, depending on the look you want. Add the pleat allowances and spaces between the pleats to determine the cut width, allowing extra fabric for seams or hems.

2. Mark the pleats and folds across the edge of the fabric. For pressed pleats, mark the fold line for the length of the pleat. See the photo for box pleats, Step 2.

3. Fold and press the pleats at the marks with the folds meeting in the center. Press the top edges only for soft pleats or the entire length for pressed pleats.

4. Baste across the top edge of the fabric to secure the pleats for a skirt or edge. Baste across the top and bottom edges for a pleated insert or panel.

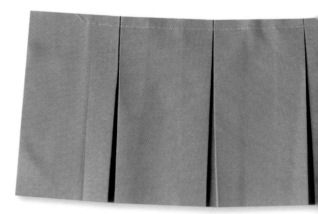

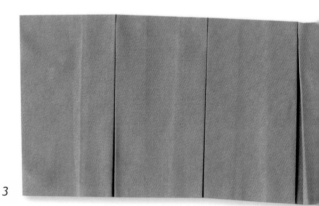

3

Knife Pleats

Basic knife pleats feature single folds pressed in the same direction. They can be wide or narrow and spaced according to the look you're trying achieve or the width of the finished project. You can stitch them across the top edge only or along the folded edges for free-hanging pleats, across both the top and bottom edges for pleated inserts or panels, or the top and bottom edges in opposite directions for twisted pleats.

Basic Knife Pleats

1. To determine the cut width of the fabric to be pleated, first determine the width of the pleat and the depth of the fold (usually half the width of the pleat). For example, if the pleat width is 1" (2.5 cm) and the fold depth is ½" (1.3 cm), the total pleat allowance

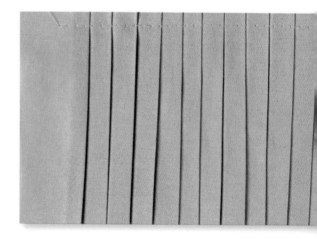

is 1½" (3.8 cm). Adjust the width or fold depth as needed to achieve the finished width of your choice. In general, wide pleats look best on larger projects such as ottomans, bed skirts, slipcover skirts, and window treatments, while smaller pleats look nice on pillows, garments, and smaller home-décor or wearable accessories.

2. Unlike box and inverted pleats where the fold lines meet in the center, a knife pleat's fold overlaps the next pleat. To ensure straight, evenly-spaced pleats, it is helpful to mark the fold and the fold-placement line on the fabric. Use a chalk pencil and clear ruler to mark the fold and placement lines across the width of the fabric. For pressed pleats, mark the entire length of the pleat; for soft folds, mark only the edge to be pleated.

3. Fold the fabric along the fold lines, aligning the folded edge with the placement line. Press the folds in place if you want pressed pleats or pin the top edges in place if you want soft folds. Baste across the edge of the fabric to secure the pleats.

4. For a pleated insert or panel, press the length of the pleats or the tops and bottoms of the pleats; then baste across both edges to secure the folds.

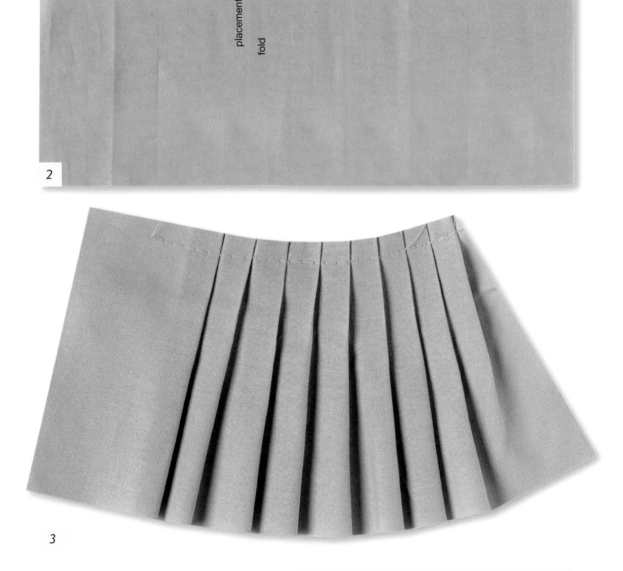

placement

fold

2

3

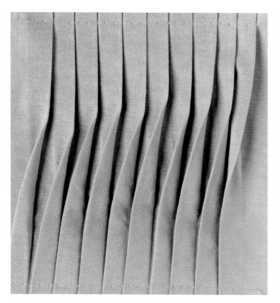

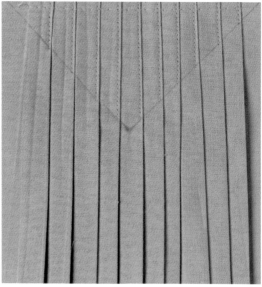

Twisted Knife Pleats

Twisted pleats add dimension as a decorative accent to inserts or panels.

1. Follow the instructions for the basic knife pleats (page 100).

2. Stitch across the top edge to secure the top of the pleats. Press the bottom of the pleats in the opposite direction and stitch in place along the edge.

Tailored Knife Pleats

Add a decorative touch to pressed knife pleats when you edge-stitch the pleats in place to create a diagonal design as the pleats are released. This technique adds interest to pleated skirts or edges on home-décor projects and garments.

1. Press the knife pleats in place along the length of each pleat.

2. Use a clear ruler and chalk or a fabric marker to draw diagonal lines as desired to create a zigzag design at the top of the pleats.

3. Stitch close to each fold from the top edge of each pleat to the marked line.

4. Remove the marked line and press.

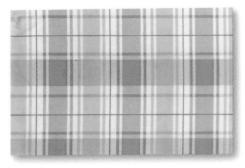

Pleated Stripes

Add a touch of surprise to pleats when you use striped or plaid fabrics. By simply folding the fabric along vertical color lines you can create inverted pleats with contrasting folds or knife pleats with contrast on the underside. This effect is also a good way to maximize or minimize a stripe's color. For best results, look for fabrics with even stripes and a repeating color order. You can achieve the same effect by piecing a vertical strip of fabric for the inside of the pleat.

For knife pleats, fold and press the fabric along the edge of one stripe. Align the folded edge with the edge of the next same-color stripe. If the stripe is too narrow to make a pleat, skip the next same-color strip and align the edge with the next one. Baste the top edges in place.

You can pleat the fabric at left so the vertical stripes appear green with a pink underside or pink with a green underside.

For inverted pleats with stripes in two alternating colors, fold the edges of two matching color stripes to meet in the center of the contrasting-color stripe. This process will minimize the color on the inside and provide contrast as shown in the photo. Press the folds and baste across the top edges. The decorator fabric at right appears predominately pink or green, depending the color used for the inside pleat.

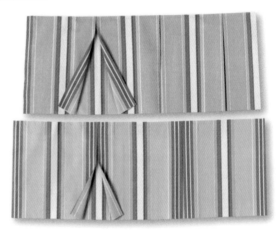

To create a contrasting, inverted pleat with strips of fabric, determine the width of the inside pleat and folds. Cut out the strip, adding ½" (1.3 cm) seam allowances to the long edges. Sew the strip between two panels of the outer fabric. Press the seam allowances toward the outer fabric.

Fold the fabric at the seams with the folds meeting in the center of the pleat. Press and baste the top edges to secure the pleats.

TWIN NEEDLE PIN TUCKS

These small raised tucks are easiest to stitch on light-to-medium-weight fabrics, and you create them by stitching with a twin needle. Twin needles are available in several needle-spacing widths—the wider the spacing, the larger the pin tuck will be. Use needles with narrow spacing on very lightweight fabrics only. For best results, also use a pin-tuck foot on your sewing machine. These feet feature grooves on the bottom of the foot that accommodate the stitched tucks and make it easy to evenly space the tucks without marking them.

You can stitch pin tucks in parallel rows or stitch them to create diamond or square designs. Because they take up a small amount of fabric, allow extra width and length when cutting out your fabric piece or panel.

1. It's easier to stitch smooth pin tucks without puckers when you make them on the cross grain of the fabric instead of the lengthwise grain. Cut the fabric panels or pieces accordingly if possible.

2. Set up your machine with a pintuck foot and a twin needle. Use a 1.6 mm–2 mm needle for lightweight fabrics or a 2.5 mm–3 mm needle for medium-weight fabric. Thread each needle from a separate spool of thread. You can use the same or differently colored threads on each side of the tuck depending on the look you want.

3. Proper thread tension is the key to successfully making raised tucks. If the tension is too loose, the fabric will lie flat between the two rows of stitching. Experiment on scraps of the fabric you will be stitching, adjusting the tension to achieve the best results. If the pin tucks are too flat, tighten the needle tension until they are raised. If the pin tucks are puckered, reduce the needle tension.

4. Once you've achieved the best tension, use a disappearing fabric marker or chalk pencil to mark the first pin-tuck placement line. Stitch along the line, creating the first pin tuck.

5. Insert the first pin tuck in the groove of the foot to stitch the next row. When you're finished stitching, press the fabric next to the pin tucks but do not press the pin tucks because they will flatten.

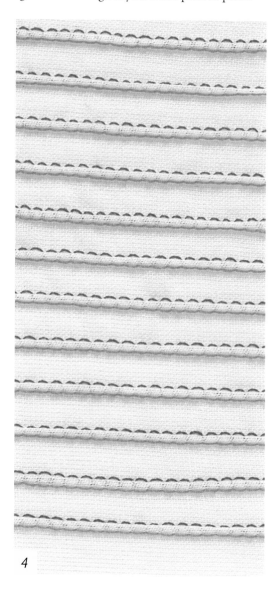

4

SINGLE NEEDLE TUCKS

You can also make pin tucks and wider tucks with a single needle and all-purpose presser foot.

1. Use a chalk pencil to mark a line for the center of each tuck on the right side of the fabric. Press each fold in place with wrong sides together.

2. Stitch each pleat ⅛" (3 mm) from the fold for pin tucks or up to ½" (1.3 cm) from the fold for wider tucks.

3. Press pin tucks next to the stitching only. Press wider tucks flat in either direction.

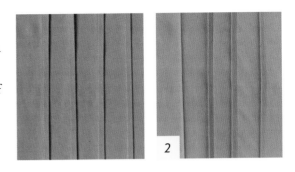

BEYOND THE BASIC TUCK

Who says tucks need to be stitched in neat parallel rows? You can have fun when you use them to create diamonds or squares, stitch part of the tuck in an opposite direction, or insert trim in the tuck. You can also tack parallel tucks together and embellish them with beads for a pretty look. Spray the fabric lightly with spray starch before making the tucks to add a crisp look and maintain the shape.

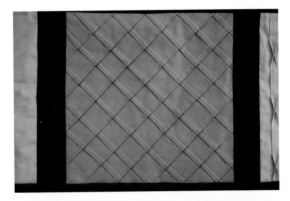

Creating Diamonds or Squares

1. Use a chalk pencil to lightly mark lines for a diamond or square pattern on the fabric. Follow the instructions for twin-needle pin tucks, opposite or single-needle tucks, above, to stitch all tucks running in the same direction.

2. Press the tucks in one direction or eliminate pressing if desired for pin tucks.

3. Stitch the tucks running in the opposite direction to complete the diamond or square design.

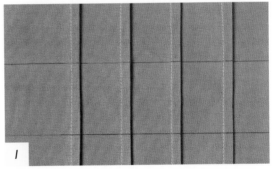

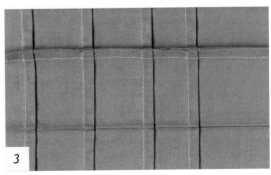

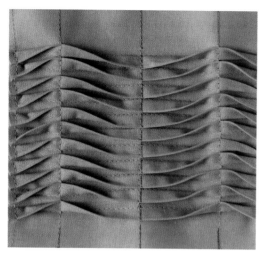
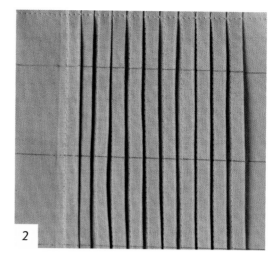

Undulating Tucks

1. Stitch parallel rows of ¼"to ½" (6 mm to1.3 cm) wide tucks. Press the tucks in the same direction. Baste the top and bottom edges in place.

2. Use a chalk pencil to mark perpendicular rows across the tucks. Stitch along the marked lines, folding each tuck in the opposite direction as you approach it and stitch it down.

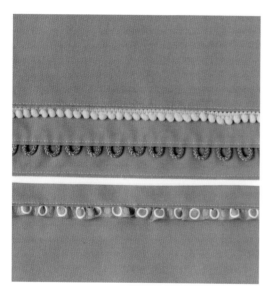

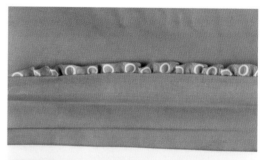

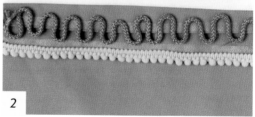

Trimmed Tucks

Add a touch of fun to all or some of the tucks on your panel when you add trim to peek out of the tuck. Consider using ribbon, small cording with a lip, rickrack, looped yarn or threads, or strips of folded fabric.

1. Mark and press each tuck to be embellished but do not stitch it in place. It is easiest to trim tucks that are ¼"to ½" (6 mm to 1.3 cm) wide.

2. Apply a strip of self-adhesive, double-sided basting tape on the inside top edge of each tuck. Adhere the bottom edge of the trim to the tape.

3. Fold the tuck back up and edge-stitch the tuck in place, securing the trim in the stitching.

Tacked Tucks

You can space these tucks across the width of your panel or stitch them in pairs with spacing between the pairs. Remember that it is necessary to make an even number of tucks for this technique.

1. Stitch parallel rows of narrow tucks. Press the tucks in each pair in opposite directions.

2. Mark the edges of the tucks at evenly-spaced intervals for tacking. Fold the edges up and tack them together at the marks.

3. If desired, stitch a bead or small button over the tacking thread.

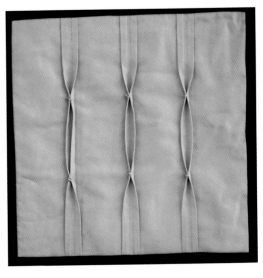

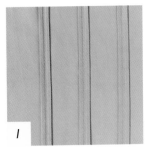

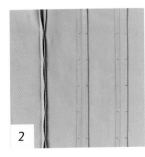

Box Tucks

These tucks have a similar appearance to box pleats, but you stitch them along the entire length instead of only at the top and bottom edges. They are easy to make and also easy to adapt to a bow tie variation.

1. Stitch parallel rows of even tucks spaced at least twice the width of the tucks.

2. Press the tucks flat and centered over the seam.

3. Mark evenly-spaced horizontal lines across the tucks. Stitch along the lines.

4. To make a bow tie, mark the edges of the box tuck in the center. Tack the edges together.

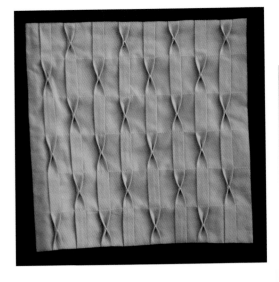

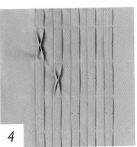

Wavy Tucks

Sewing tucks in a curve can be tricky, but it's easier when you use fusible tricot interfacing to secure the curved tuck.

1. Cut a piece of fusible tricot that is 2" (5 cm) larger than the desired size for the finished panel. Cut a piece of light-to-medium-weight fabric in the same width but 2" (5 cm) longer than the tricot.

2. On the nonfusible side of the tricot, draw a wavy line 1" (2.5 cm) from the top edge. If desired, draw the wavy line on a piece of cardboard and use it as a template.

3. Place the fabric wrong-side up on a pressing surface; then place the interfacing fusible-side down on the fabric, aligning the top edges. Press the top edge up to, but not over, the marked line.

4. With the interfacing side up, stitch along the marked line.

5. With the fabric right side up, fold approximately ⅛" (3 mm) of fabric over the stitched line and press.

6. On the interfacing side, draw the next wavy line and stitch. Turn the fabric right side up and repeat Step 5. Repeat to mark, stitch, and press one line at a time until you finish the panel.

SLITS

A creative surface embellishment doesn't necessarily have to be on top of the surface. You can create interesting effects when you layer and stitch nonfraying knit fabric and then cut straight or wider slits to reveal the fabric beneath.

Use this fun technique to make panels for piecing into shirts, throws, pillows, and other accessories.

1. Layer two contrasting panels of interlock knit fabrics and pin the edges together. Draw parallel stitching lines spaced ½" to 1" (1.3 to 2.5 cm) apart if you plan to cut straight slits or 1½" (3.8 cm) apart if you plan to cut wider slits. Stitch along the lines.

2. Use a fabric marker and draw a line centered between each set of stitched lines. Begin and end the marked lines at least ½" (1.3 cm) from the top and bottom edges. Use sharp, pointed scissors and cut along each line, cutting through the top layer of fabric only.

3. For wider slits, trim each side of the slit's opening up to ¼" (6 mm) wide.

4. Sew the panels together with traditional seams or serging. Because the edges won't ravel, you can sew or serge wrong sides together as shown on the panels with wider slits.

2

3

Fabric Manipulation Projects

Trapunto Floor Pillow

Add extra seating to any room or put your feet up when you make a comfy floor pillow. Faux trapunto stitching and trims add the perfect finishing touches.

MATERIALS

Fabrics

1 yd (0.9 m) of 54" (137.2 cm)-wide decorator fabric for top and bottom panels

⅔ yd (0.6 m) of coordinating 54" (137.2 cm)-wide decorator fabric for the sides

¾ yd (0.5 m) of 36" (91.4 cm)-wide muslin

Other Supplies

3 yd (2.7 m) of 1" (2.5 cm) ball fringe

four 1½" (3.8 cm)-diameter buttons with shanks

36" × 36" (91.4 × 91.4 cm) square of high-loft batting

3 lb (1.4 kg) of polyester fiberfill

self-adhesive double-sided basting tape

Finished Size

30" (76.2 cm) in diameter × 8" (20.3 cm) high

Cutting

1. For top panel, cut a 36" × 36" (91.4 × 91.4 cm) square from the decorator fabric, centering motifs as desired. Also cut a 36" × 36" (91.4 × 91.4 cm) square of the batting and muslin.

2. For the bottom panel, cut one 32" × 32" (81.3 × 81.3 cm) square. To cut it into a circle, fold the square in half, then in half in the other direction, with the wrong side out. Using a clear ruler and fabric pen, place the zero at the point of the folded square. Make a mark at the edge of one side 15½" (39.4 cm) from the point. Keeping zero constantly at the point, gradually move the ruler across the fabric to mark an arc 15½" (39.4 cm) from the point.

3. For the sides, cut two 9" × 49½" (22.9 × 125.7 cm) strips across the width of the fabric.

Assembly

Note: Use a ½" (1.3 cm) seam allowance and sew seams with right sides together.

1. On a large flat surface, layer the muslin, batting, and fabric right side up. Begin in the center and pin the layers together, pinning around each motif to be stitched.

3. Begin in the center and stitch along the outline of each motif. Press lightly to remove wrinkles.

4. Center the bottom panel on the top panel and trace around the edges of the bottom panel. Cut the top panel out on the traced line. Evenly space and sew the buttons to the top panel 6" (15.2 cm) from the center.

5. Use basting tape to adhere the ball fringe header to the edge of the top panel, aligning the header and edge with the ball fringe toward the inside.

Note: It's easier to keep the header smooth along the edge with basting tape than with pins.

1

6. Sew the short edges of the side pieces together. Press the seams open. Pin the sides to the top panel or adhere with basting tape. Sew the sides to the top. Repeat for the bottom, leaving a 10" (25.4 cm) opening for turning and stuffing.

7. Turn the pillow cover right side out and press the edges. Press the opening seam allowances under. Stuff firmly and slip-stitch the opening closed.

Yo–yo Door Hanger

Add a decorative accent to a door knob or drawer pull when you layer yo-yos made with fabric strips to make a fanciful reversible hanger. Embellish ribbon flowers with buttons, and finish it off with a cord-and-tassel hanging loop.

1

MATERIALS

Fabrics

¼ yd (0.2 m) each of three contrasting fabrics

Other Supplies

16" (40.6 cm) length of ⅜" (1 cm)-diameter twisted cord

1¼ yd (1.1 m) of ⅞" (2.2 cm)-wide grosgrain ribbon

4" (10.2 cm)-long tassel with hanging loop

Cutting

1. For the large 7" (17.8 cm)-diameter yo-yo, cut two 2¼" × 21" (5.7 × 53.3 cm) strips from the one fabric and one 2½" × 21" (1.3 × 53.3 cm) strip from a contrasting fabric.

2. For the two medium 4" (10.2 cm)-diameter yo-yos, cut two 3½" × 21" (8.9 × 53.3 cm) strips from the remaining fabric.

3. From the ribbon, cut two 21" (53.3 cm) strips.

Assembly

Note: Use a ¼" (6 mm) seam allowance and sew seams with right sides together.

1. To make the large yo-yo, sew the contrasting-fabric strip between the two main fabric strips. Press the seams open. Press the strip in half lengthwise with wrong sides together. Follow the instructions for the fabric-strip yo-yo (page 94).

4

2. To make the medium yo-yos, cut two 3½" × 21" (8.9 × 53.3 cm) strips. Follow instructions for the fabric-strip yo-yo to make two medium yo-yos.

3. To make each ribbon flower, sew the short ends of one strip of ribbon together. Sew a basting stitch along one long edge. Pull the threads to gather the ribbon tightly and knot the thread ends together.

4. Fold the cording in half to make a loop. Tape the ends to the top of the tassel loop. Position the cording on the large yo-yo with the loop extending 3½" (8.9 cm) above the top edge. Glue the bottom of the cording loop and the top of the tassel loop to the yo-yo with permanent fabric adhesive.

5. Glue or sew a ribbon flower to the center of each medium yo-yo. Glue a button or layered buttons to the center of each ribbon flower.

5

Textured—blocks Wall Hanging

Combine solid-color fabrics and fabric texturing techniques like pleats and tucks to make the blocks for this wall hanging. Make it larger or smaller by adding more blocks to the width or length.

MATERIALS

Fabrics

1½ yd (1.4 m) each of two solid-color 45" (114.3 cm)-wide cotton fabrics for blocks

2½ yd (2.3 m) of contrasting solid-color 45" (114.3 cm)-wide cotton fabric for block accent, sashing strips, border, backing, and binding

40" × 40" (101.6 × 101.6 cm) square of fusible batting

Other Supplies

buttons: one 1" (2.5 cm)-diameter; two ½" (1.3 cm)-diameter

six glass seed beads

general sewing supplies

Finished Size

36" × 36" (91.4 × 91.4 cm)

Note: Make four blocks in one block color fabric and five in the remaining block color fabric.

Block 1: Knife pleats

1. Cut a 10½" × 30" (26.7 × 76.2 cm) rectangle of fabric.

2. Mark the fabric crosswise into 1" (2.5 cm) and ½" (1.3 cm) parallel lines. Fold along the lines and press to make ½" (1.3 cm)-wide knife pleats as shown in the instructions for knife pleats (page 100).

3. Trim the pleated fabric to a 9½" × 9½" (24.1 × 24.1 cm) square. Baste the pleats in place along the top and bottom edges.

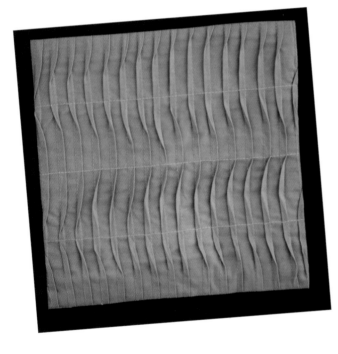

Block 2: Undulating tucks

1. Cut a 10½" × 22" (26.7 × 55.9 cm) rectangle of fabric.

2. Follow the instructions for basic tucks (page 105) to make 16¼" (41.3 cm)-wide tucks spaced ½" (1.3 cm) apart across the width of the fabric. Trim the block to a 9½" × 9½" (24.1 × 24.1 cm) square, with the pleats centered.

3. Press the tucks to one side and baste across the top and bottom of the panel. Mark a horizontal stitching line across the center of the panel. Mark two more horizontal stitching lines 2¼" (5.7 cm) above and below the center line.

4. Stitch along the center line. For the lines above and below the center line, stitch from the opposite direction, folding the tucks in the opposite direction as you approach them. Press to set the undulating design.

Block 3: Diagonal undulating tucks

1. Cut a 10" × 24" (25.4 × 61 cm) rectangle of fabric.

2. Follow the instructions for basic tucks (page 105) to make 24" (61 cm)-wide tucks spaced ⅜" (1 cm) apart across the width of the fabric. From the center of the block, press 12 tucks to the right and 12 tucks to the left. Trim the block to a 9½" × 9½" (24.1 × 24.1 cm) square.

3. Mark diagonal lines from corner to corner across the block. Stitch from the top right corner to the bottom left corner without changing the direction of the pleats. Stitch from the top left corner to the bottom right corner, turning each tuck in the opposite direction as you approach it.

4. Press the tucks in the resulting left and right triangles toward the center.

5. Sew a 1" (2.5 cm)-diameter button to the center of the block.

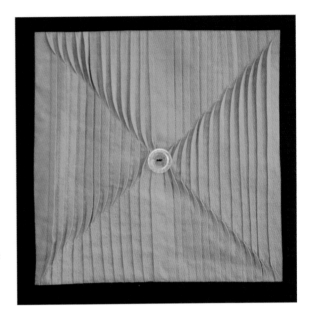

Block 4: Square tucks

1. Cut a 14" × 18" (35.6 × 45.7 cm) rectangle of fabric.

2. Follow the instructions for basic tucks (page 105) to make nine ¼" (6 mm)-wide tucks spaced 1" (2.5 cm) apart across the width of the fabric. Press the tucks in one direction.

3. Turn the fabric and make a ¼" (6 mm)-wide tuck in the lengthwise center of the fabric. Make another lengthwise tuck 1" (2.5 cm) above the center tuck and one 1" (2.5 cm) below it. Trim the block to a 9½" × 9½" (24.1 × 24.1 cm) square with the pleats centered.

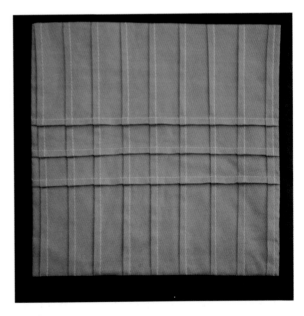

Block 5: Inverted pleats

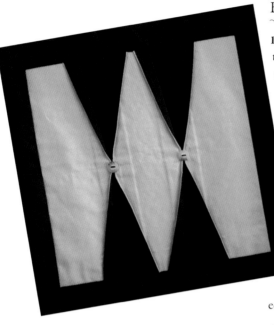

1. Cut three 3½" × 10" (8.9 × 26.7 cm) rectangles from the main fabric. Cut two 3½" × 10½" (8.9 × 26.7 cm) rectangles from the contrasting fabric.

2. Sew the two contrasting strips between the main fabric strips. Press the seams toward the main fabric strips.

3. Follow the instructions for inverted pleats (page 100) to make two contrasting, inverted pleats and press the pleats in place.

4. Mark a line vertically across the center of the panel and stitch on the line. Press the top and bottom edges of each pleat open.

5. Trim the block evenly to a 9½" × 9½" (24.1 × 24.1 cm) square. Baste across the top and bottom edges, securing the folded-back pleats.

6. Sew a ½" (1.3 cm)-diameter button to the center of each pleat.

Block 6: Twisted knife pleats

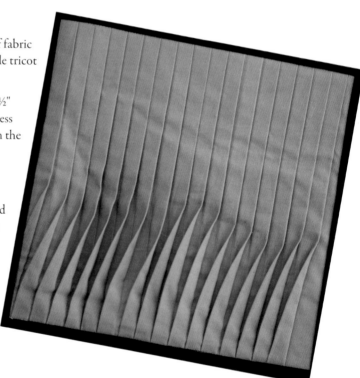

1. Cut a 10½" × 30" (26.7 × 76.2 cm) rectangle of fabric and a 9½" × 9½" (24.1 × 24.1 cm) square of fusible tricot interfacing.

2. Mark the fabric crosswise into 1" (2.5 cm) and ½" (1.3 cm) parallel lines. Fold along the lines and press to make ½" (1.3 cm)-wide knife pleats as shown in the instructions for knife pleats (page 100).

3. Trim the pleated fabric to a 9½" × 9½" (24.1 × 24.1 cm) square. Place it on top of the fusible tricot square and fuse the top of the pleated square to the interfacing. Baste the pleats in place along the top edge.

4. Turn the pleats in the opposite direction on the bottom edge and fuse it to the interfacing. Baste the pleats in place along the bottom edge.

Block 7: Tacked tucks

1. Cut a 10½" × 14" (26.7 × 35.6 cm) rectangle of fabric.

2. Follow the instructions for tacked tucks (page 107) to make two ¼"(6 mm)-wide tucks spaced ⅜" (1 cm) apart in the center of the fabric. Make another set in the same dimensions 2¼" (5.7 cm) from each side of the center, measured from stitching line to stitching line.

3. Trim the block to a 9½" × 9½" (24.1 × 24.1 cm) square, centering the sets of tucks.

4. Press each set of tucks open. Mark the edges at 3½" (8.9 cm) from the top and bottom edges. Hand tack the edges together at the marks, adding a seed bead as you stitch.

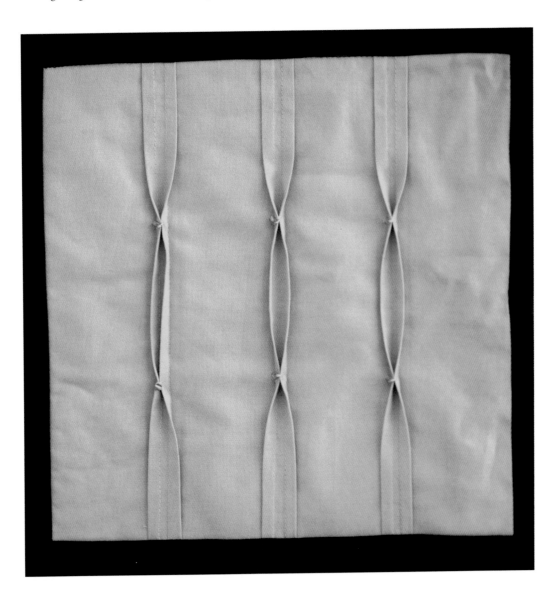

Block 8: Diagonal tucks

1. Cut a 30" × 30" (76.2 × 76.2 cm) square of fabric

2. Make nine ¼" (6 mm)-wide tucks spaced 1¼" (3.2 cm) apart across the width of the fabric. Press the tucks in one direction.

3. Turn the fabric and make nine ¼" (6 mm)-wide tucks spaced 1¼" (3.2 cm) apart across the length of the fabric. Press the tucks in one direction.

4. With the resulting squares on point, trim the block to a 9½" × 9½" (24.1 × 24.1 cm) square

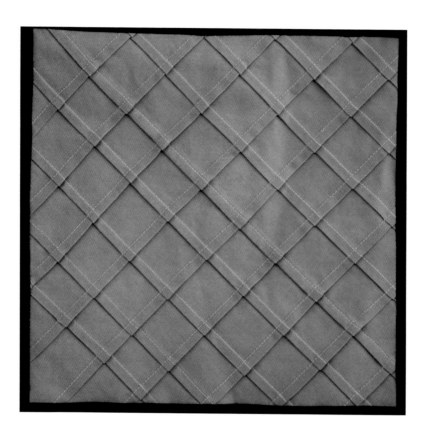

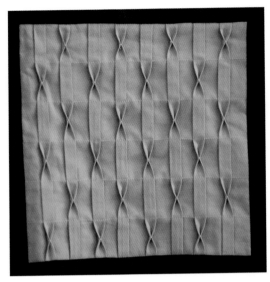

Block 9: Box Tucks and Bow Ties

1. Cut a 10½" × 20" (26.7 × 50.8 cm) rectangle of fabric.

2. Follow the instructions for box tucks (page 107) to make and press eight ½" (1.3 cm) tucks spaced 1" (2.5 cm) apart. Trim the block to 9½" × 9½" (24.1 × 24.1 cm) square with the pleats centered. Use a fabric marker or chalk pencil and clear ruler to draw a line across the block, 1¾" (4.5 cm) from the top edge. Draw parallel lines across the block at 1½" (3.8 cm) increments, ending 1¾" (4.5 cm) above the bottom edge. Stitch on the lines.

3. Baste across the top and bottom of the block ¼" (6 mm) from the edges. Follow the instructions for bow ties (page 107) to make alternating bow tie segments.

Assemble Wall Hanging

Note: Use a ¼" (6 mm) seam allowance, sew seams with right sides together, and press all seams to one side after stitching.

1. From the contrasting fabric, cut six 2" × 9½" (5 × 24.1 cm) strips and two 2" × 31½" (5 × 80 cm) strips for the sashing, two 2" × 31½" (5 × 80 cm) strips for the side borders, two 2" × 36" (5 × 91.4 cm) strips for the top and bottom borders, one 40" × 40" (101.6 × 101.6 cm) square for the backing, and 2¼ (5.7 cm)-wide bias strips pieced to 4¼ yd (3.9 m).

2. Arrange the blocks in three rows of three blocks each. Assemble each row by sewing the side edges of the blocks to the long edges of the 9½" (24.1 cm)-long sashing strips. Press the seams to one side.

3. Sew the 31½" (80 cm)-long sashing strips to the top and bottom edges of the center row. Sew the top and bottom rows to the remaining edges of the sashing strips.

4. Sew a side-border strip to each side of the pieced top. Sew the top and bottom borders in place.

5. Layer the backing wrong side up, the batting, and the pieced top right side up and centered. Follow the batting manufacturer's instructions to fuse the layers together.

6. Press the binding strip in half lengthwise with wrong sides together. Beginning in the center of one edge, pin the binding to the wall hanging's top with raw edges even, folding at the corners to form mitered corners. To end the binding, cut the excess strip 2" (5 cm) beyond the beginning end. Turn the short end under 1" (2.5 cm) and wrap it around the beginning end. Stitch the binding in place ¼" (6 mm) from the edge. Wrap the folded edge of the binding to the back of the wall hanging. Stitch in the ditch from the front, securing the folded edge in the stitching.

7. To finish, stitch in the ditch on both sides of the sashing strips. Hang as desired.

ARTISTIC ELEMENTS

If you love to sew and embellish, options abound for indulging your inner artist with techniques that go beyond the sewing machine. Dyes, fabric paints, bleach, and ink all make it easy to alter the color of your fabric for embellishing or for adding designs with brushes, stencils, or stamping. Or grab some favorite fabric motifs and an array of other embellishments to make a fabric collage.

Techniques

COLOR—ADDING IT IN AND TAKING IT OUT

It's always fun to experiment with color, whether you're adding it with dye or fabric paint, blocking the dye with resist, or stitching or binding the fabric and removing it with bleach. These techniques can result in interesting—even unpredictable—fabric surfaces that provide fabulous backgrounds for adventurous stitching and other embellishments.

Bleach Techniques

Grab that bleach from your laundry room and use it for a creative adventure when you remove color from fabric. Liquid bleach is ideal for designing reverse tie-dye effects as shown on the pillow (page 134), and you can use bleach-gel pens to stencil or draw free-hand details. The key to working with bleach is to use natural-fiber fabrics, and most important, to experiment. Fabrics will react to the bleach differently; even two denim fabrics can require different soaking times and can yield different shades of blue as you remove the color.

Liquid Bleach

If you don't leave the fabric in the bleach long enough, the color change will be slight, and if you leave it in too long, you will lose the interesting definitions, and the fabric will become fragile and prone to ripping.

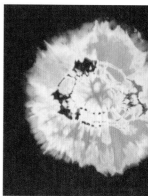

For example, in the photos shown, the same denim fabric was left in the bleach for two different lengths of time, with the first swatch left in for 15 minutes. It shows the color fading but not much definition. For this denim, the ideal soaking time was 25 minutes; the folds left interesting details, and the fabric showed several shades of blue.

The reverse tie-dye technique is the same as regular tie-dye, except you use bleach instead of dye. You can gather the fabric with a gathering stitch for straight designs or bind it with rubber bands for round designs. Experiment with crinkling, folding, pleating, and other fabric-manipulation techniques to see the interesting results you can achieve. If you will launder and machine-dry the fabric, prewash and dry it before bleaching.

1. Bind the fabric to be bleached with rubber bands or stitching. Twist the fabric to create folds and wrap the rubber bands tightly.

Or fold a strip of fabric several times, stitch a gathering stich along the center and pull the thread ends to tightly gather the fabric; knot the thread ends. Loose gathers will not be as defined as tight ones.

2. Fill a glass bowl or measuring cup with liquid bleach to a depth that will cover the piece you want to bleach.

3. Place the fabric in the bleach, making sure the bleach doesn't extend above the top rubber band for bound fabric. For gathers, submerge the entire piece or only one side, depending on the look you want. Watch the color removal carefully to determine the soaking time.

4. Wear rubber gloves to remove the fabric from the bleach and hold it under running water to stop the bleaching process. Remove the rubber bands or stitching and rinse the fabric well. Let it dry flat or place it in a dryer.

Bleach pen

These pens, available in the detergent section of grocery and home-improvement stores, contain a thick gel. You can easily control it with the pen-like applicator on one end or the brush-like applicator on the other end. Use it as you would a pencil or paintbrush to write or make designs.

To use it with a stencil:

1. Apply stencil adhesive to the wrong side of the stencil; then adhere it to the right side of the fabric.

2. Work from the outer edges to the inside using either end of the pen to apply the gel to the stencil openings. Allow it to set until you have removed the desired amount of color; this process will take longer than liquid bleach.

3. Rinse the fabric well and allow it to dry.

WORKING WITH DYES, PAINT, AND INK

Fabric absorbs dyes, while paint and ink sit on the surface, but all can be combined with hand or machine stitching to achieve a myriad of embellishments. Consider adding some of the following artistic touches to your repertoire of adventurous embellishment techniques:

Stenciled or Stamped Designs.

Apply fabric paint within the openings of a stencil or apply fabric paint or ink to the fabric with a stamp. Let the paint dry and stitch around the outline with a straight stitch.

Using a Stamp as a Template.

This technique is an easy way to add an outline to fabric for stitching, appliqué, quilting, trapunto, or fiber etching. Apply paint or ink to the surface of the stamp; then apply it to poster board or heavyweight paper. Cut out the motif. Place it on fabric and trace around the outline. Stitch on the outline and embellish the motif as desired.

Binding Fabric.

Refer to the bleach instructions (page 126) to bind fabric with a rubber band or gather it with stitching but immerse it in dye instead of bleach. Be sure to follow the instructions on the dye packet or bottle for preparing the dye bath and rinsing the fabric. Embellish the dyed fabric design with machine or hand stitches.

ETCHING FABRIC

Embellishing fabric isn't always about adding to the surface; sometimes it involves removing fibers from the surface. This technique is easy to do with a liquid gel called Fiber Etch that dissolves cellulose (plant) fibers. Use it to create burnout areas on fabrics that are 100% cotton, linen, or rayon or to create sheer effects on fabric blends that combine yarns made with cellulose fibers with wool, silk, or synthetic yarns. You can use it alone or combine it with a machine-embroidered, satin-stitched, or painted outline.

Basic Fiber Etch Instructions

1. Wash and dry the fabric to remove sizing, if necessary.

2. Pin or tape the fabric to newspaper.

3. Apply a thin layer of gel on the area to be removed, scratching it into the fabric with the tip of the bottle. *Note:* If you accidentally get unwanted gel spots on the fabric, sprinkle it with baking soda or wash immediately with soap and water.

4. Dry the gelled areas with a hairdryer.

5. Remove the fabric from the newspaper and place it right side down on a pressing surface. Press with an iron set on medium heat until the area with the gel becomes brown and brittle.

6. Rinse under running water, rubbing the fabric gently until the etched fibers fall away.

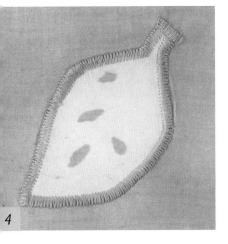

Outline Stitching and Fiber Etch

Whether you want to create a burned out area or a sheer one, you can combine any machine-embroidered or satin-stitched design that creates an outline with Fiber Etch.

1. Use polyester thread in the needle and the bobbin. Rayon, cotton, and all-purpose threads will dissolve when you apply the gel.

2. Use a digitized design for machine embroidery or trace the outline of the design to be stitched onto the fabric.

3. Embroider or satin-stitch the design

4. Follow the instructions for basic Fiber Etch above to apply the gel within the stitched outline and to complete the etching process.

Stamps and Fiber Etch

Foam stamps and clear stamps for fabric are ideal for use with Fiber Etch, with or without fabric paint.

Stamps with Paint

1. To etch areas of a design stamped with paint, look for stamps with cut-out design areas that are open and large enough for etching. If you're using cellulose-fiber fabric, be sure the open areas aren't too close together or the entire area may be removed and leave an unwanted hole in the fabric. Avoid small or intricate details.

2. Use a foam brush and apply a thin layer of fabric paint to the stamp. Immediately press it onto the fabric and lift it straight up. Let the paint dry.

3. Apply Fiber Etch in the detail openings, keeping it slightly inside the painted outline.

4. Follow the instructions for basic fiber etch (page 129) to apply the gel within the stitched outline and to complete the etching process. A cellulose fabric (a) with have cut-out areas. A blended fabric (b) will have sheer areas.

4a

4b

Stamps with Fiber Etch Only

1. Stamps used with Fiber Etch only are generally best used on blended fabrics for sheer effects. Avoid small details that will fill in when you apply the gel.

2. Use a foam brush and apply a thin layer of gel to the stamp. Immediately press it onto the fabric and lift it straight up.

3. Follow the instructions for basic fiber etch (page 129) to dry and press the gel areas. Because it is difficult to see if you have stamped the gel evenly at first, you can evaluate the design when it begins to turn brown. If desired, repeat the process of applying gel and drying it to fill in. The designs will show up when you dye the fabric.

FABRIC COLLAGE

No rules or boundaries exist when it comes to creating a fabric collage; anything goes. Just gather some favorite fabrics and trims and fire up your imagination to get started. Whether you choose to make a soft or quilted fabric collage or a canvas wall hanging, this technique is a great way to use your fabric stash!

Planning

Your collage can have a theme, or it can simply be a collection of fabrics and trims you like. Even though the design possibilities are limitless, chances are you'll be happier with your finished project if you begin with a general plan. To get started, consider some of the following ideas:

Decide on the type of foundation you want to use. The stretched canvas wall hanging (page 138) was stitched onto canvas-like, multi-purpose cloth and then stretched onto a frame, resulting in a flat surface. You can also create a soft or quilted surface when you stitch your collage onto muslin or other foundation cloth.

Do you want your collage to have a theme? Vacations, nature, pets, a favorite photograph, or a hobby can be a starting point. Gather fabrics, trims, and images that reflect this topic.

A sketch can be helpful. It doesn't have to be precise, just a general idea of what you'd like to do. For example, for the "Nature's Harmony" fabric collage (page 138), I knew I wanted to include elements of nature from my garden and favorite vacation spot as well as an image of my dog and bird appliqués. With these ideas in mind, I drew a very rough sketch of where I would place the appliqués and photo transfer.

Plan some larger fabric pieces for the background. You will be covering the edges and some of the fabric, but it makes it easier to place smaller pieces without the foundation fabric showing through.

Vary the size and scale of cut-out fabric motifs to keep the eye moving across the piece. Too many same-size pieces aren't as distinctive as contrasting-size pieces.

Create your own designs in addition to using cut-out motifs. Not an artist? Consider taking photographs of flowers or birds, enlarging them and tracing them onto fusible web for transfer to fabric. Or cut an 8½" × 11" (21.59 × 27.9 cm) rectangle of multi-purpose cloth and use your printer to print the image to make a raw-edge appliqué.

Gather fabrics in a variety of prints and colors that you like together. You can have a color theme or combine a mixture of colors. Either way make sure you have contrasting colors and print sizes.

Use a variety of threads for stitching; variegated threads can add interest to outlines, and heavy thread weights will stand out nicely for adding details or outlines.

Have fun with trims. Add snippets of trims or sew on buttons or beads. For the wall canvas, I layered small pieces of suede and loosely-woven silk and then added grommets to the centers for a touch of fun and dimension.

I also couched yarn onto the saguaro cactus to indicate spines and then wrapped the base with flower trim for a touch of whimsy.

Assembling the Collage

1. Mark the finished size of your collage, plus seam allowances for a soft collage or the frame's depth for a wall canvas.

2. Arrange the background pieces on the fabric or canvas, making sure you have covered the edges.

3. Pin and then edge-stitch the background pieces in place.

4. Prepare and add your cut-out motifs and any appliqués. As you work, evaluate the balance of the pieces on the background fabrics. Fill in more background pieces if desired. When you are satisfied with the arrangement, pin and then edge-stitch the pieces in place.

5. Embellish the finished piece with detail stitching, couching, and trims as desired.

Bleach—motifs Floor Pillow

MATERIALS

Fabrics

1½" yd (1.4 m) of 60" (152.4 cm)-wide denim fabric

Other Supplies

24" × 24" (61 × 61 cm) pillow form

two 2" × 25" (5 × 63.5 cm) strips of fusible interfacing

buttons: two 1" (2.5 cm)-diameter for closure; assorted for embellishment

beads for embellishment

thread: all-purpose and heavy weight

liquid bleach

glass measuring cup

wide rubber bands

Finished Size

24" × 24" (61 × 61 cm)

Instructions

1. From the denim, cut four 16" × 16" (40.6 × 40.6 cm) squares for the front, two 16" × 25" (40.6 × 63.5 cm) rectangles for the back and eight 5" × 29" (12.7 × 73.7 cm) strips for the flange.

2. Referring to the instructions for reverse tie dye (page 124), gather the center of each fabric square and use rubber bands to tightly bind the fabric 1" (2.5 cm) and 4" (10.2 cm) from the center. Soak the bound areas in the bleach. Remove the fabric from the bleach and rinse and dry it. Press each flange strip in fourths lengthwise and sew a basting stitch down the center of the strip. Knot the thread ends together on one end. Pull the threads on the opposite end to tightly gather the strip.

3. Trim each square with the bleached motif to 13" × 13" (33 × 33 cm) with the motif centered. Sew the squares together in two rows of two squares each. Press the seams open.

4. Follow Step 2 to create a reverse-tie-dye motif in the center of the pieced panels.

(continued)

5. Using the bleached design as a guide, accent the lines with machine stitches and heavy-weight thread.

6. Add buttons or beads as desired to complement the stitching.

7. To add the flange, press the flange strips in half lengthwise with wrong sides together. Mark the lengthwise center on the raw edges of each folded strip. Pin the strips in place, matching the center marks to the piecing seams. Sew the strips in place, beginning and ending the stitching ½" (1.3 cm) from the corners. To miter each corner, fold the fabric in half diagonally with right sides together and border edges even. Mark a line from the end of the denim corner to the outside edge of the flange strips. Stitch along the marked line. Press the seams open and stitch or glue gimp trim over them to cover the raw edges.

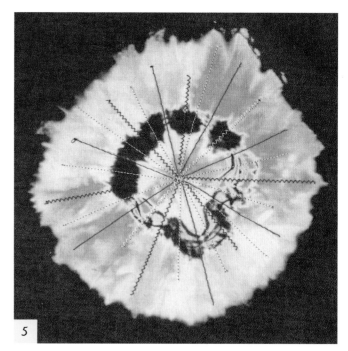

5

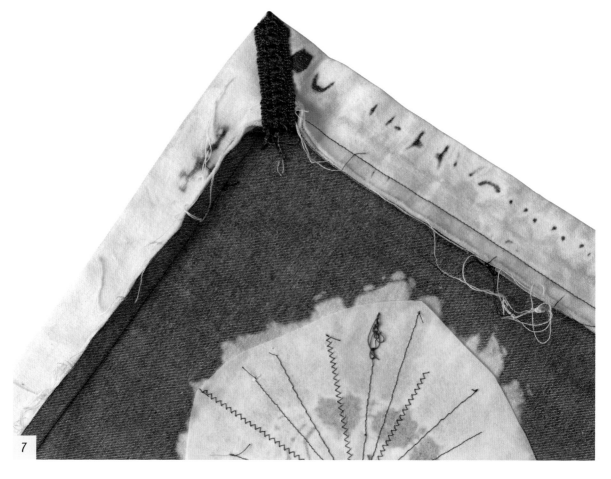

7

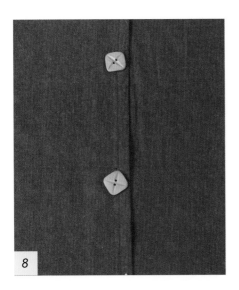

8. To assemble the back panel, fuse an interfacing strip to the wrong side of one long edge of each panel. Press the interfaced edges under 2" (5 cm) and topstitch them in place. Overlap the hemmed edges to form a 25" × 25" (63.5 × 63.5 cm) square and baste the overlapping edges together. Mark two evenly spaced button-hole and button placements. Stitch the buttonholes and sew the buttons in place.

9. With raw edges even, sew the edges of the front and back panels together, being careful not to catch the flange in the stitching.

10. Insert the pillow form through the back opening and button the closure.

Nature's Harmony Wall Canvas

Cover a stretched canvas with a fabric collage inspired by some of your favorite things. I love nature and the outdoors, so I chose two of my favorite places as sources of inspiration—the desert and colors of the Southwest and my own garden in Illinois. They may be hundreds of miles apart, but here they harmoniously exist, expressed in fabric. For fun, I added birds, butterflies, and a photo transfer of my dog Lucy in a costume that makes me smile. Think of the things that make you smile; that's a good place to begin.

MATERIALS

Fabrics

12" × 24" × ¾" (30.5 × 61 × 1.9 cm) stretched canvas or 12" (30.5 cm) and 24" (61 cm) stretcher strips to make frame

½" yd (0.5 m) of multi-purpose canvas cloth for foundation

fabric scraps: large and small floral and graphic motifs, solids, batiks

Other Supplies

trim scraps

thread: all-purpose, heavyweight and decorative

embroidered motifs (optional)

stamps and ink or paint (optional)

staple gun and staples

general sewing supplies

Finished Size

12" × 24" × ¾" (30.5 × 61 × 1.9 cm)

Cutting and Assembly

1. From the multipurpose cloth, cut a 16" × 28" (40.6 × 71.1 cm) rectangle. Draw a 12" × 24" (30.5 × 61 cm) outline in the center of the rectangle to indicate the outline of your canvas front. Draw another line ¾" (1.9 cm) outside the outline to mark the sides; you will wrap the rest of the canvas to the back.

2. Plan the pieces for the main background of your collage, selecting randomly cut pieces of fabric and rough-cut motifs. Arrange the pieces on the canvas as desired, extending the pieces to cover the marked sides.

3. When satisfied with the background layout, fine-tune the shapes as desired, cutting around the edges of motifs and smoothing curves and edges. Pin and then edge-stitch the pieces in place.

4. Referring to the instructions for fabric collage (page 131), add the next layer of trimmed-fabric motifs and any motifs you design and cut freehand. I drew and cut out cactus, birds, and a large flower in addition to the trimmed-fabric motifs. I printed a photo of my dog Lucy onto canvas and cut it out and machine-embroidered two floral motifs. Pin and then edge-stitch the additional pieces in place.

5. Set your machine for free-motion stitching and stitch all pieces, following the design lines of the motifs and adding free-form stitching as desired. When you finish, look at your design; if some areas still need something, cut out and add another motif. Or plan to embellish the area with stamping, couching, trims, or dimensional-embroidery motifs.

6. Referring to the photo for ideas, add the finishing touches that you determined in Step 5.

7. Assemble the stretcher strips if using them to make a frame. Center the finished collage on the frame or canvas and wrap the edges to the back. Securely staple the edges in place.

Painted, Etched, and Dyed Scarf

Have some fun with etching, paints, and dye when you make a scarf with etched sheer motifs. The key to success is using fabric such as the featured batiste-like, Azeta cotton fabric. Woven with cotton fibers in one direction and polyester fibers in the other direction, the polyester resists both the etching gel and dye, resulting in sheer, white, etched areas that contrast with the dyed surface.

MATERIALS

Fabric

½ yd (0.5 m) of 52" (133 cm)-wide, white, cotton/polyester-blend fabric

Other Supplies

Fiber Etch

foam leaf stamps with detail openings: 2¼" × 3¾" (5.7 × 9.5 cm); 1½" × 2¾" (3.8 × 7 cm)

green fabric paint

one packet of powdered turquoise dye

1" (2.5 cm)-wide foam brush

plastic to cover the work surface

hairdryer

general sewing supplies

Finished Size

9" × 52" (22.9 × 133 cm)

Preparation:

1. Wash and air dry the fabric to remove any sizing, if necessary. Cut a 10" (25.4 cm)-wide strip across the width of the fabric.

2. Press under a doubled ¼" (6 mm) hem on both long edges of the fabric. Topstitch the hems in place. Repeat for the short edges.

Create the Etched Design

Refer to the Fiber Etch Basics instructions for the following steps:

1. Use the large leaf stamp to apply five painted leaf motifs on one end of the hemmed scarf, reapplying the paint to the stamp between motifs. Begin 1½" (3.8 cm) above the bottom edge for the first stamp and position the top stamp 13" (33 cm) above the bottom edge. Use the tip of the Fiber Etch bottle to apply Fiber Etch to the openings of the stamped design. Dry the piece, press it, and rinse it to remove the cotton fibers, resulting in sheer openings.

2. Apply Fiber Etch to the small leaf stamp and stamp four motifs among the large leaves, reapplying the gel to the stamp between motifs. Dry and press it, checking to make sure you have filled in the stamp design to your satisfaction.

3. Rinse the piece to remove the cotton fibers, resulting in sheer leaf motifs.

4. Repeat Etching Steps 1 to 3 on the opposite end of the scarf.

Finish

1. Follow the manufacturer's instructions to prepare the dye bath. Dampen the scarf and immerse it in the dye. Follow the dye manufacturer's instructions for stirring and length of time required for dyeing, checking the depth of the color periodically. Remove the scarf from the dye and rinse it.

2. Let the scarf air dry. Press it on medium heat.

3. Using all-purpose sewing thread, machine stitch along the outline of each painted leaf motif.

1

2

3

Credits and Sources

Tablet cover, page 34: Amy Butler's fabrics from Westminster Fibers; Steam a Seam 2, fusible-web tape from Warm Company; Peltex stabilizer and featherweight interfacing from Pellon; and Nancy Zieman's Tablet Keeper Shapers from Clover.

Monogrammed table topper, page 40: Circular sewing attachment and PE-Design Next embroidery software from Brother; Solvy + stabilizer and threads from Sulky; WoolFelt from National Nonwovens.

Appliqué embroidery, page 30: Anita Goodesign's Jacobean appliqué from Amazing Designs.

Dimensional flowers, page 31: Starbird's 3D Flowers from www.embroidery.com.

Appliquéd chair cushion, page 54: Anna Maria Horner's Innocent Crush fabric from Westminster Fibers; Poly-fil from Fairfield Processing Corp. Steam a Seam 2 fusible web from Warm Company.

Raw-edge appliqué pillow, page 60: Amy Butler's Lark collection and Ty Penningon's Expressions collection from Westminster Fibers; Steam a Seam 2 fusible web from Warm Company; Soft Touch Pillow form from Fairfield Processing Corp.; thread and stabilizer from Sulky; Wrap 'n Fuse Piping from Clover.

Dimensional-appliqués throw, page 64: WoolFelt from National Nonwovens; novelty-print bias tape and rickrack from Michael Miller Fabric; waxed button thread from Dritz.

Decorative zippers, page 83: Fashion zippers from Coats & Clark.

Grommet samples, page 79: Featured in Sew News, March 2012.

Embellished jacket, page 86: Sticky Fabri-Solvy and Solvy water-soluble stabilizers from Sulky.

Embellished motifs pillow, page 88: Jute cord from May Arts; appliqué and edge trim from Expo International; Soft Touch Pillow Form from Fairfield Processing Corp.

Pillow with couched design, page 90: Jute cord from May Arts; appliqué and edge trim from Expo International; Soft Touch Pillow Form from Fairfield Processing Corp.

Trapunto floor pillow, page 110: Wonder Tape (basting tape) from Dritz; ball fringe from Expo International; high-loft batting and Poly-fil polyester fiberfill from Fairfield Processing; buttons from JHB International; Ty Pennington's Impressions collection fabric from Westminster Fibers.

Yo-Yo door hanger, page 114: Amy Butler's fabrics from Westminster Fibers; tassel and twisted cord from Expo International.

Textured-blocks wall hanging, page 116: Kona cotton fabrics from Robert Kaufman; fusible batting from Fairfield Processing Corp.

Reverse tie-dye floor pillow, page 134: Denim fabric from Robert Kaufman; Soft Touch Pillow Form from Fairfield Processing Corp.; dual duty heavy and all-purpose threads from Coats.

Nature's harmony wall canvas, page 138: Multipurpose cloth from Roc-lon; 12-wt. cotton thread and 30-wt. Blendables thread from Sulky; heavy-duty thread from Coats & Clark.

Painted, etched, and dyed scarf, page 140: Azeta cotton-blend fabric and Fiber Etch from Silkpaint.

Sources:

Amazing Designs, www.amazingdesigns.com

Brother, www.brother.com

Coats & Clark, www.coatsandclark.com

Clover, http://www.clover-usa.com

Dritz/Prym Consumer USA, www.dritz.com

Embroidery.com, www.embroidery.com

Expo International, www.atreasurenest.com

Fairfield Processing Corp., www.poly-fil.com

JHB International, www.buttons.com

May Arts, www.mayarts.com

Micheal Miller Fabrics, www.michaelmillerfabrics.com

National Nonwovens, www.nationalnonwovens.com

Pellon, www.pellonideas.com

Robert Kaufman, www.robertkaufman.com

Roc-lon, www.roc-lon.com

Silkpaint, www.silkpaint.com

Sulky of America, www.sulky.com

Warm Company, www.warmcompany.com

Westminster Fibers, www.westminsterfibers.com

About the Author

Carol Zentgraf is a designer, writer, and editor specializing in sewing, fabrics, and decorating. She has a degree in art and interior design from Drake University and especially enjoys incorporating a variety of artistic techniques into her fabric projects. Carol has worked in the craft and sewing industries as both a designer and editor for more than 30 years and is the author of eight books. She is also a regular contributor to several magazines and web sites. Carol lives in Illinois with her husband Dave and her sewing supervisor—Lucy, an English Bulldog.

Index

A

Appliqué embroidery, 30–31
Appliqué techniques
  designs & fabrics for, 46
  dimensional, 50–51
  finished edge, 49
  fusible web backing, 47
  raw-edge, 50, 60–63
  reverse, 52–53
  stabilizer sheets, 48
  templates, 46–47

B

Background quilting, 26
Basting tape, 17
Bias tape designs on stabilizer, 77
Bleach-motifs project, 134–137
Bleach techniques, 126–127
Bobbin work, 28–29
Box pleats, 99
Buttons, 78–79

C

Chair cushion appliqué project, 54–59
Collages, 131–133
Color, adding & removing, 126–130
Cording, 17
Couching, 72–74
Crazy quilting stitches, 20–22
Cutwork, 32

D

Decorative stitches
  bobbin work, 28–29
  crazy quilting, 20–22
  digitized machine, 30–33
  free-motion, 26–27
  heirloom, 23–25
Dimensional appliqué, 50–51, 64–69
Door hanger project, 114–115
Drawn thread work, 24

E

Echo stitching, 27
Edge embellishments, 84–85
Embellished motifs pillow project, 88–89
Etching fabric, 129–130
Eyelets, 80–81

F

Fabric tube embellishments, 76–77
Fabric tube turners, 17
Fabrics, 10
Fagoting, 25
Finished edge appliqué, 49
Fusible web, 16, 47

G

Gathers, 96–98
Grommets, 80–81

H

Hemstitching, 23–24

I

Inserts, gathered, 98
Interfacings, 16
Inverted pleats, 100

J

Jacket project, 86–87

K

Knife pleats, 100–102

L

Layering, stitching for, 27

M

Machine embroidery, digitized, 30–33
Monogramming, 33, 40–43

N

Notions for surface designs
  buttons, 78–79
  on edges and seams, 84–85
  grommets and eyelets, 80–81
  zippers, 82–83

O

Outlining, 26

P

Piping, making, 84–85
Pleats, 99–102
Projects
  chair cushion, 54–59
  door hanger, 114–115
  jacket, 86–87
  pillows, 60–63, 88–91, 110–113, 134–137
  scarf, 140–141
  table topper, 40–43
  tablet cover, 34–37
  throw, 64–69
  tote, 38–39
  wall hangings, 116–123, 138–139

R

Raw-edge appliqué, 50, 60–63
Reverse appliqué, 52–53

S

Scarf project, 140–141
Seam embellishments, 84–85
Sewing machine feet, 14–15
Sewing machine needles, 12–13
Slits, 109
Spray adhesives, 17
Stabilizers, 16, 48, 77
Stencils/stamps, 128, 130
Stripes, pleated, 103

T

Table topper project, 40–43
Tablet cover project, 34–37
Templates, 46–47, 58–59, 69
Thread painting, 27
Threads, 10–11
Throw project, 64–69
Tote project, 38–39
Trapunto, 94–95
Trapunto floor pillow project, 110–113
Trims, using, 11, 74–76, 90–91
Tucks, 104–108

W

Wall hanging projects, 116–123, 138–139
Welting, making, 84–85

Y

Yarns, 11
Yo-yo gathers, 96–97, 114–115

Z

Zippers, 82–83